Study Guide for Burger's
Personality

Fourth Edition

Thomas L. Wilson
Bellarmine College

Brooks/Cole Publishing Company

I(T)P® An International Thomson Publishing Company

Pacific Grove • Albany • Belmont • Bonn • Boston • Cincinnati
Detroit • Johannesburg • London • Madrid • Melbourne • Mexico City
New York • Paris • Singapore • Tokyo • Toronto • Washington

Sponsoring Editor: *Faith B. Stoddard*
Editorial Associate: *Nancy Conti*
Production Coordinator: *Dorothy Bell*

Cover Design: *Roy R. Neuhaus*
Cover Art: *David Park/Whitney Museum of American Art*
Printing and Binding: *Malloy Lithographing*

COPYRIGHT © 1997 by Brooks/Cole Publishing Company
A division of International Thomson Publishing Inc.
I(T)P®   The ITP logo is a registered trademark under license.

For more information, contact:

BROOKS/COLE PUBLISHING COMPANY
511 Forest Lodge Road
Pacific Grove, CA 93950
USA

International Thomson Editores
Seneca 53
Col. Polanco
C. P. 11560 México, D. F., México

International Thomson Publishing Europe
Berkshire House 168-173
High Holborn
London WC1V 7AA
England

International Thomson Publishing GmbH
Königswinterer Strasse 418
53227 Bonn
Germany

Thomas Nelson Australia
102 Dodds Street
South Melbourne, 3205
Victoria, Australia

International Thomson Publishing Asia
221 Henderson Road
#05-10 Henderson Building
Singapore 0315

Nelson Canada
1120 Birchmount Road
Scarborough, Ontario
Canada M1K 5G4

International Thomson Publishing Japan
Hirakawacho Kyowa Building, 3F
2-2-1 Hirakawacho
Chiyoda-ku, Tokyo 102
Japan

All rights reserved. No part of this work may be reproduced, stored in a retrieval system, or transcribed, in any form or by any means—electronic, mechanical, photocopying, recording, or otherwise—without the prior written permission of the publisher, Brooks/Cole Publishing Company, Pacific Grove, California 93950.

Printed in the United States of America

10 9 8 7 6 5 4 3

ISBN 0-534-34561-1

COVER ART
Park, David
Four Men   1958
Oil on canvas
57 x 92 in. (144.8 x 233.7 cm)
Collection of Whitney Museum of American Art
Purchase, with funds from an anonymous donor
59.27

To my wife,
the most wonderful personality I know

Preface

To the Student

This study guide has been designed to help you succeed in your course on personality. The study guide does not replace the textbook material. The activities provided in these pages supplement and expand on the textbook. With effective regular use of the study guide you will master the most important facts, concepts, and key issues discussed in the text. It will help you grow in your knowledge of the fundamental approaches to personality and their applications in many settings. Finally, it will help you prepare yourself for examinations by strengthening your understanding of the material and confidence in your knowledge.

Each chapter of the study guide corresponds to a chapter in the textbook. There are several sections in each chapter that provide different learning activities to help you move beyond mere passive reading and rote memorization to take command of the textbook topics. The sections are: Chapter Outline, Learning Objectives, Important Concepts, Programmed Review, Multiple Choice Questions, Integrative Questions, and Evaluative Questions. Working on each of these sections will increase your learning on several levels, some at the level of facts and applications and some at the levels of analysis, integration, and critical evaluation. Take time to do these learning activities. They are based on cognitive learning strategies that research has shown to lead to better comprehension and retention.

The following is a description of the learning activities involved in each section and guidelines on how to use each one effectively. Of course, only you can determine for yourself how to best use this study guide, how much time and effort you can put into study, and what sections work best for you. We urge you to give each activity a try before you pass judgment on its effectiveness.

Organized around learning objectives, the study guide has been designed to exercise and elaborate your knowledge. A fundamental property of the human mind is that information more deeply processed is more accurately and reliably retained in memory. One suggestion is to begin with a brief review of the *structure* of the textbook chapter given in the Chapter Outline, and then a *careful study* of the Learning Objectives before opening the textbook to begin to study. The remainder of the study guide sections are recommended to achieve deeper processing of the textbook material once it has been read.

Chapter Outline

Each chapter of the study guide begins with an outline of chapter topics. Organizing your knowledge is a key to good learning. By reviewing the Chapter Outline prior to reading, you can get an overall sense of the organization of the textbook material as a first step toward forming relationships among topics and organizing your knowledge. Having the topical organization in mind prior to study improve one's comprehension of the textbook over simply reading straight through.

Learning Objectives

Following the Chapter Outline you will find a list of Learning Objectives. At first glance the list may appear long and tedious because of its detail and resemblance to essay questions. Work on these objectives in small steps; do not try to master the entire list in one long study session. The Learning Objectives make up a comprehensive list of the *abilities* you should acquire in your mastery of the textbook material. When you can demonstrate to yourself that you have acquired these abilities, then you can be confident in your full mastery of the material.

The Learning Objectives should be carefully reviewed *before* reading each textbook chapter or chapter section. You are not expected to have these abilities yet; just read about them. Once the Learning Objectives are firmly in mind, the material you read in the textbook will jump out at you and engage you in active purposeful reading. Some students find it helpful to create their own short essay-type test to monitor their understanding as they read and study the textbook. Most successful students have developed the ability to self-monitor as they study; the learning objectives can serve this function. After studying some textbook material, go back to the Learning Objectives and use them as short essay questions. Write your answers as best you can. If you don't have the answer to a question, then go back to the textbook for more study. As a diagnostic tool, answering the Learning Objectives will provide you with useful feedback about the abilities that need more of your attention and further study.

Important Concepts

A list of the most important and highlighted concepts from the textbook chapter is provided for quick reference to definitions and for easy study of the most basic form of knowledge: facts and concepts. It is important to do more than just memorize facts. Try to *relate* concepts to one another as you study. For example, how does a topic in the textbook relate to other topics under the same section heading? Be able to define and give an example of each concept. When people generate their own examples of new information, the knowledge is more deeply processed and memory is enhanced. Simply write out your own example for each concept in the list. For more information about a given concept, the page number from the textbook is given where you can find the concept discussed.

Some students may find it helpful to create flash cards of these concepts and their definitions, or flash cards of the concepts and examples, to take with them in their daily activities. Repetition is a fundamental strategy that the mind uses to improve memory, so repetitive learning through flash cards can be beneficial if you use them effectively! Avoid including too much information on any given card. Although it may seem better to have a lot of information memorized from flash cards, too much information defeats the purpose of rote rehearsal that flash cards provide. Also, avoid learning from 20 or 30 flash cards at a time. Again, too much at one time can interfere with memory rather than improve it. It is better to take 5 or 6 cards with you each day to master during free time or study time before doing more.

Programmed Review

The Programmed Review is also designed to help you monitor your knowledge after reading in the textbook. At first glance you may not like this section because it looks like fill-in-the-blank questions. It is a given that students would rather listen to a three hour sermon than do fill-in questions. But the Programmed Review is more than filling in blanks and it is surprisingly easy to use and highly effective as a learning strategy. It helps you master the important concepts that are at the heart of the material. So try it!

After reading in the textbook, close the book and keep it nearby. Turn in the study guide to the Programmed Review. Using a sheet of paper to cover the answer written immediately below each statement, pulling it down to just reveal the statement and nothing more. Then try to write down an appropriate response; do not skip over these statements passively. After responding, move the cover sheet down to reveal the answer. If you are correct, move on to the next statement. If you are incorrect, then immediately turn to the page in the textbook given to the right of the answer to review the given concept.

Multiple Choice Questions

After studying the textbook, familiarizing yourself with the major concepts, and completing the Programmed Review, you are ready to test your general knowledge of the chapter material. The Multiple Choice questions are provided as another diagnostic tool to prepare for exams in the course. While it is recommended that you study the textbook in manageable sections rather than all in one sitting, the Multiple Choice section should be completed in one brief session. Take this test before moving on to sharpen your knowledge with the open-ended essay questions in the last two sections.

Multiple Choice questions come in two varieties: definitional/conceptual questions and application questions. The definitional/conceptual questions test your knowledge of the facts and definitions of concepts. The application questions help you determine how well you can apply your knowledge in everyday life. The answer key is given immediately following the last question. The appropriate page numbers in the textbook are given with each answer so that you can check your understanding.

Integrative Questions

A higher level of knowledge is the level of integration at which individual facts and concepts are synthesized and interrelated to strengthen your command of the material. Integrative questions require you to discover the deeper meaning and relationships among major topics within each chapter and across chapters. These questions and the Evaluative Questions in the last section are not tests. They should be considered learning exercises because your answer is likely to be uniquely based on your understanding.

Evaluative Questions

Perhaps an even deeper level of understanding is the ability to assess and critically evaluate the issues and concepts that you have learned from careful study of the textbook. The Evaluative Questions will focus your critical thinking skills on selected topics. Like the Integrative Questions, there are no specific answers except those found in your careful study of the textbook. Exercise your knowledge by considering each question one at a time. The write out your answer using the appropriate terms and good reasoning. Be sure to *support* all of your assertions with information presented in the textbook. When you have finished writing your essay answer, go back into the textbook and evaluate the answer for yourself. While you assess the goodness of your answer you will discover yourself learning even more.

We encourage you to study effectively by making good use of the learning activities in this study guide. Your success in learning is our goal. By exercising and elaborating your growing knowledge of the theories of personality, relevant research, and their applications, you will be prepared to demonstrate to your instructor what you know with confidence on course exams. More importantly, you will increase your learning skill and you will become better prepared to apply your knowledge of personality in your life and career. Best wishes for learning!

T. W.
J. B.

Contents

1	What is Personality?	1
2	Personality Research Methods	11
3	The Psychoanalytic Approach: Freudian Theory, Application, and Assessment	21
4	The Freudian Approach: Relevant Research	31
5	The Psychoanalytic Approach: Neo-Freudian Theory, Application, and Assessment	39
6	The Neo-Freudian Theories: Relevant Research	49
7	The Trait Approach: Theory, Application, and Assessment	57
8	The Trait Approach: Relevant Research	67
9	The Biological Approach: Theory, Application, and Assessment	77
10	The Biological Approach: Relevant Research	85
11	The Humanistic Approach: Theory, Application, and Assessment	93
12	The Humanistic Approach: Relevant Research	103
13	The Behavioral/Social Learning Approach: Theory, Application, and Assessment	111
14	The Behavioral/Social Learning Approach: Relevant Research	123
15	The Cognitive Approach: Theory, Application, and Assessment	133
16	The Cognitive Approach: Relevant Research	143
17	Some Concluding Observations	149

Chapter **1**

What is Personality?

Chapter Outline

The Person and the Situation
Defining Personality
Six Approaches to Personality
    Two Examples: Aggression and Depression
Personality and Culture
The Study of Personality: Theory, Application, Assessment and Research
    Theory
        Genetic Versus Environmental Influences
        Conscious Versus Unconscious Determinants of Behavior
        Free Will Versus Determinism
    Application
    Assessment
    Research

Learning Objectives

1. State whether behavior is influenced by the environment or reflects contributions by the individual. Explain why the situation is important to personality psychologists.

2. Define personality in your own words. Explain how psychologists answer the question, "What is personality?" Give examples to illustrate the two major parts of the definition of personality offered in the textbook.

3. Describe what is meant by "intrapersonal processes." Discuss the two major factors that determine our individual character.

4. Give six brief answers to the question, "What are the sources of consistent behavior and intrapersonal processes for the individual?" according to the six major approaches to personality. List by name and distinguish the six major approaches to personality.

5. Discuss the role culture plays in personality. Define and distinguish between individualistic cultures and collectivist cultures. State how behaviors take on different meanings depending on the culture.

6. List the four components of the study of each approach to personality that are necessary for a complete understanding of personality. Give examples of your own of each component.

7. Discuss the specific goals that theories of personality attempt to accomplish. Describe three issues related to the nature of human personality that theorists must consider in their formulations. Give an example of each issue and state how most psychologists think about each one.

8. Distinguish and give an example of the sign approach and the sample approach. State which general approaches to personality theory make use of each assessment technique.

9. List the major purposes for conducting personality research.

Important Concepts

personality (p. 4)
intrapersonal processes (p. 4)
individual differences (p. 4)
individualistic culture (p. 12)
collectivist culture (p. 12)
theory (p. 13)
application (p. 13)
research (p. 13)
assessment (p. 13)
sign approach (p. 18)
sample approach (p. 18)

psychoanalytic approach (p. 5)
biological approach (p. 5)
behavioral/social learning approach (p. 5)
trait approach (p. 5)
humanistic approach (p. 5)
cognitive approach (p. 5)
free will (p. 15)
determinism (p. 15)

Programmed Review

Many psychologists concern themselves with how people typically respond to _____ .

environmental demands   p. 2

The author of the textbook defines personality as consistent _____ and intrapersonal processes originating within the individual.

behavior patterns   p. 4

_____ include all the emotional, motivational and cognitive processes that go on inside the individual.

intrapersonal processes   p. 4

The _____ approach argues that differences in behavior result from inherited predispositions and physiological processes.

biological   p. 5

According to the _____ approach, personal responsibility and feelings of self-acceptance are key causes of personality.

humanistic   p. 5

One way psychologists evaluate which approach to personality is correct is through _____ .

research   p. 6

The _____ approach to personality focuses on individual differences in the stability of behavior.

trait   p. 7

Psychologists who take the behavioral/social learning approach to personality would suggest that aggressive behavior is learned because it has been _____ .

rewarded   p. 7

The humanistic approach to personality suggests that problems like aggressive behavior result when something interferes with _____ .

natural growth processes   p. 7

How you respond to a situation is a function of how you interpret it. This is a basic argument of the _____ approach to personality.

cognitive   p. 8

People in _____ cultures tend to think of themselves as independent and unique.

individualistic   p. 12

Most theories presented in your textbook come from research in _____ cultures.

individualistic   p. 13

Included in _____ are psychotherapy, education, and behavior in the work place.

applications   p. 13

Personality psychology is, after all, a _____ .

science   p. 13

B. F. Skinner argued that our behavior is not freely chosen but rather the direct result of _____ to which we've been exposed.

environmental stimuli   p. 15

Cognitive therapists try to change the way their clients _____ .

process information   p. 16

Assessment is the way in which psychologists from a particular personality theory _____ concepts identified in the theory.

measure   p. 16

When test are given to people and a trained psychologist interprets the results, the approach to assessment being used is the _____ .

sign approach   p. 18

Multiple Choice Questions

1. When we look closely at the reactions of people to the same situation, we see
    a. that people are more alike than they are different.
    b. evidence that most people behave in typical ways.
    c. characteristic differences between people begin to emerge.
    d. each individual's personality is overwhelmed by the demands of the situation.

2. Which of the following questions would a personality psychologist ask?
    a. Why are some people prone to addiction?
    b. How can the success of college students be predicted?
    c. Why do some people help in traumatic situations while others don't?
    d. all of the above

3. Psychologists use the term *individual differences* to refer to
   a. the consistent behavior patterns individuals display across time.
   b. the interpersonal processes that originate within the individual.
   c. the consistent behavior patterns individuals display across situations.
   d. both a and c

4. When she is at home, Rebecca is very well behaved and polite. But Rebecca's mother is troubled when she learns that her daughter is rude and unkind at school. According to the psychoanalytic approach to personality, Rebecca's behavior
   a. can be identified along a continuum of personality characteristics.
   b. is the result of unconscious mental activity.
   c. results from conditioning and expectations.
   d. is a reaction to differing feelings of self-acceptance.

5. Refer to Question #4 above. According to the trait approach to personality, Rebecca's behavior
   a. can be identified along a continuum of personality characteristics.
   b. is the result of unconscious mental activity.
   c. results from conditioning and expectations.
   d. is a reaction to differing feelings of self-acceptance.

6. Zeek and Zack are having a debate about which personality theory is correct. Zeek says that differences in behavior are due to differences in the way people process information. Zack disagrees by saying that patterns of behavior are inherited and people differ because their physiological make-up is different. Zeek seems to follow the _____ approach while Zack probably follows the _____ approach.
   a. humanistic; biological
   b. behavioral/social learning; psychoanalytic
   c. cognitive; biological
   d. cognitive; trait

7. The results of most studies of personality
   a. cannot be explained by psychoanalytic theory.
   b. support the behavioral/social learning approach over other approaches.
   c. are useless for evaluating which theory of personality is most supported.
   d. can be explained within each of the approaches.

8. The approach to personality that explains aggressive behavior as an expression of frustration resulting from unsatisfied basic needs is the
   a. psychoanalytic approach.
   b. biological approach.
   c. behavioral/social learning approach.
   d. humanistic approach.

9. The approach to personality that explains aggressive behavior as unconscious impulses turned outward on other people is the
   a. psychoanalytic approach.
   b. trait approach.
   c. cognitive approach.
   d. humanistic approach.

10. Which of the following approaches to personality points to genetic predispositions as the reason for consistent patterns of behavior?
    a. trait approach
    b. biological approach
    c. behavioral/social learning approach
    d. cognitive approach

11. Which of the following approaches to personality explains aggression by how situations are perceived and interpreted?
    a. psychoanalytic approach
    b. trait approach
    c. biological approach
    d. cognitive approach

12. According to the psychoanalytic approach, depression is
    a. a malfunction of the brain.
    b. predictable from earlier episodes of depression.
    c. anger turned inward.
    d. low self-esteem.

13. For people who are depressed, a psychologist following the behavioral/social learning approach to personality would probably examine
    a. the best predictors of emotional level.
    b. the environment surrounding the depressed person.
    c. what depressed persons say about themselves.
    d. the genetic susceptibility to depression.

14. Looking at the beliefs and attributions of depressed persons is what a psychologist of the _____ approach would do.
    a. humanistic
    b. cognitive
    c. trait
    d. behavioral/social learning

15. People in collectivist cultures differ from people in individualistic cultures in that
    a. they are more interested in cooperation than competition.
    b. they are more interested in competition than cooperation.
    c. they place great emphasis on people's accomplishments.
    d. they tend to think of themselves as unique.

16. Suppose you meet a new person on campus from a culture different from your own. You soon discover that the your new friend has difficulty understanding what you mean by "self-esteem." You conclude that your friend probably comes from
    a. an individualistic culture.
    b. a collectivist culture.
    c. a nonindustrial culture.
    d. a small family.

17. Which of the following is not among the four components necessary for understanding the study of personality?
    a. theory
    b. assessment
    c. insight
    d. application

18. Of the following approaches, which ignores inherited (genetic) influences the most?
    a. cognitive
    b. biological
    c. psychoanalytic
    d. trait

19. The theorist who said that people assume they are aware of the reasons for their behavior although they often are not aware of them held to the _____ approach.
    a. behavioral/social learning
    b. psychoanalytic
    c. biological
    d. humanistic

20. To apply personality research to practical concerns, industrial psychologists
    a. help people decide on careers that correspond to their aptitudes.
    b. identify characteristics of children in the classroom.
    c. design working environments to meet the needs of employees.
    d. help people overcome their personal problems.

21. The self-report inventory is an example of _____ in the study of personality.
    a. assessment
    b. research
    c. application
    d. belief

22. The sample approach to personality assessment is used
    a. by psychoanalytic psychologists to discover unconscious impulses.
    b. in the behavioral/social learning approach to measure overt behavior.
    c. for discovering whether the basic needs of the individual are being met.
    d. in none of the above.

Answers to Multiple Choice Questions

1.	c, 2	11.	d, 8	21.	a, 17
2.	d, 3	12.	c, 10	22.	b, 18
3.	d, 4	13.	b, 11		
4.	b, 5	14.	b, 11		
5.	a, 5	15.	a, 12		
6.	c, 5	16.	b, 12		
7.	d, 6	17.	c, 13		
8.	d, 7	18.	a, 15		
9.	a, 6	19.	a, 15		
10.	b, 7	20.	c, 16		

Integrative Questions

1. What is the generally agreed-upon answer to the question of whether our behavior is shaped by the situation or by the kind of person we are? Give three reasons for the answer to this question.

2. Write a two-paragraph short story about a situation in which individuals react differently to the same event. Give examples in the story of reactions that are the result of situational factors and distinguish these from reactions that are the result of intrapersonal processes.

3. It is stated in the text that each of the major theories of personality can be placed into one of the six general approaches. Turn to the Table of Contents in the textbook and create a list of the major theories by name and categorize each on by approach.

4. Think of a person you know who is aggressive. State in your own words how each of the six general approaches to personality explain that person's behavior.

5. For each of the three dichotomies that follow, draw a line representing a continuum with poles indicating the two extreme positions given in the dichotomy. Then place each of the six general approaches to personality along each continuum according to your understanding of the chapter. If an approach makes no distinction, then place it in the center of the continuum.
    (1) genetic versus environmental influences
    (2) conscious versus unconscious determinants of behavior
    (3) free will versus determinism

6. Give an example of one kind of application of personality theory from two different approaches of your own choosing. In what ways is the application different across the two approaches? In what ways are they similar?

7. Discuss the major purposes of research in personality psychology. Contrast the kinds of questions addressed by research within three of the general approaches to personality.

Evaluative Questions

1. Do psychologists agree on a single definition of personality? What should psychologists look at to study personality? State one advantage and one disadvantage of differing theoretical viewpoints in the field of personality.

2. Restate briefly the story of the blind men and the elephant. Why is the blind men analogy only partially applicable to the six approaches to personality?

3. Consider how each of the six general approaches to personality would explain unwanted aggressive behavior in an adolescent. From the basic tenets of each approach, which of the approaches holds the most promise for eliminating the aggressive behavior? Explain your answer.

4. Each of the six approaches to personality gives a different explanation for depression. State three possible answers to the question of which approach is correct in explaining the causes of depression.

5. What does it mean to say that personalities exist within a cultural context? Give your own reasons for why culture is important in understanding personality. Which of the six general approaches is best suited for explaining culture's role in personality? Why?

6. State the general goals of scientific theory. In your own estimation, how well do theories of personality do in meeting those goals?

7. Contrast your own view about the determinants of behavior with those of Freud and Skinner. Are people aware of the causes of their behavior? Why or why not?

Chapter **2**

Personality Research Methods

Chapter Outline

The Hypothesis-Testing Approach
    Theories and Hypotheses
    Experimental Variables
    Manipulated Versus Nonmanipulated Independent Variables
    The Case Study Method
        Disadvantages of the Case Study Method
        Advantages of the Case Study Method
Statistical Analysis of Data
    Statistical Significance
    Correlation Coefficients
Problems to Look for When Examining Research
    Experimental Confounds
    Comparison Groups
    Prediction Versus Hindsight
    Replication
Personality Assessment
    Reliability
    Validity
        Face Validity
        Congruent Validity
        Discriminant Validity
        Behavioral Validation

Learning Objectives

1. Distinguish among speculation, expert opinion, and empirical research as ways we come to understand personality. State how the hypothesis-tesing approach makes possible strong evidence in support of a theory.

2. Describe the four major steps of the hypothesis-testing approach. Define and state the distinction between theories and hypotheses.

3. Define with an example each of the two characteristics of good theories. Explain how psychologists test the adequacy of a theory, including with what kinds of questions they begin their research.

4. Define and give an example of independent and dependent variables. State what each variable is used for in an experiment. Identify each of these variables in research hypotheses.

5. Explain the difference in the research process between the use of a manipulated independent variable and a nonmanipulated independent variable. State the kinds of conclusions that can be drawn from research using each kind of independent variable.

6. Give an example of the case study method indicating who is studied with this method and how data are collected. State the goals achieved using the case study method.

7. Discuss the advantages and disadvantages of the case study method. List four occasions when the case study method is a useful research tool.

8. Define the meaning of statistical significance, including the role of probability in statistical decisions. Describe two situations in which one would and would not conclude the research results are statistically significant.

9. Identify the appropriate use of the correlation coefficient. Discuss the possible outcomes of a correlation analysis, the direction and strength of the coefficient, and its meaning.

10. Summarize four general problems to look for when examining research in personality. For each problem explain how the problem can make an experiment weak or difficult to interpret.

11. State what is meant by "personality assessment." Give examples of areas of psychology in which assessment is necessary.

12. Explain how we can determine a good test from a bad one. Discuss the concept of reliability and give an example of a measure that is not reliable.

13. Explain how we can determine if a test score measures what it is we want to measure. Discuss the concept of validity and explain the difference between predictive validity and construct validity.

14. Distinguish between congruent and discriminant validity. State the purpose of establishing each of these kinds of validity.

15. Discuss and give an example of behavioral validation.

Important Concepts

expert opinion (p. 20)
empirical research (p. 21)
theory (p. 22)
independent variable (p. 24)
dependent variable (p. 25)
manipulated independent variable (p. 27)
nonmanipulated independent variable (p. 28)
experimental confound (p. 35)
comparison group (p. 36)
replication (p. 38)
reliability (p. 39)
test-retest reliability (p. 39)
internal consistency (p. 40)
validity (p. 40)
congruent validity (p. 41)
discriminant validity (p. 41)
behavioral validation (p. 42)

hypothesis-testing (p. 21)
parsimonious (p. 22)
hypothesis (p. 22)
interaction (p. 26)
case study method (p. 29)
statistical significance (p. 32)
correlation coefficient (p. 33)
positive correlation (p. 34)
negative correlation (p. 34)
prediction (p. 37)
hindsight (p. 37)
hypothetical constructs (p. 40)
construct validity (p. 41)
face validity (p. 41)

Programmed Review

Because theories alone only provide part of the picture of personality, most psychologists want strong evidence from _____ .

empirical research   p. 21

Most personality research begins with a _____ .

theory   p. 22

Unless a theory can generate _____ , it may be of little use to scientists.

testable hypotheses   p. 22

The variable that determines how the groups in an experiment are divided is the _____ variable.

independent   p. 24

When the effects of one independent variable depends on the level of another independent variable, the result is called _____ .

an interaction   p. 26

The use of _____ independent variables is required when an independent variable exists without the experimenter's intervention.

nonmanipulated   p. 28

In the case study method, instead of reporting the results of statistical analyses, the investigators describe their _____ of what the person did and what it means.

impressions   p. 29

One problem with the case study method is the problem of _____ from any one case to other people.

generalizing   p. 30

Because of naturally occurring _____ in the dependent variable of any given study, one does not expect that the data will turn out the same for different experimental conditions.

variation   p. 32

The _____ is the appropriate statistic when we want to understand the relationship between two measures.

correlation coefficient   p. 33

The value of the correlation coefficient can ranges from _____ .

1.00 to -1.00   p. 34

When another variable is allowed to vary with the independent variable in an experiment, the problem that results is called _____ .

an experimental confound   p. 35

The process of _____ involves repeating experiments to obtain an effect more than once.

replication   p. 38

Researchers typically rely on a statistical significance level of _____ .

.05   p. 33

A test has good _____ when it measures consistently.

reliability   p. 39

A test is _____ when all of the items on the test measure the same thing.

internally consistent   p. 40

The extent to which a test measures what it is designed to measure is called _____ .

validity   p. 40

Demonstrating that a test accurately measures the test taker's level on a construct established the test's _____ validity.

construct   p. 41

Multiple Choice Questions

1. Personality theorists who use empirical research to support their theory make use of
   a. sophisticated speculation about patterns of behavior.
   b. expert opinion almost exclusively.
   c. the hypothesis-testing approach.
   d. direct observation of people in their natural surroundings.

2. In what order do personality researchers take steps to discover the nature of personality?
   a. generate hypotheses, evaluate data, speculate
   b. generate hypotheses, collect data, evaluate data
   c. collect data, evaluate data, speculate
   d. speculate, collect data, generate hypotheses

3. Most personality researchers today are unlike Sigmund Freud in that
   a. they speculate about the where behaviors come from.
   b. modern researchers use case studies to understand personality.
   c. they typically work with theories that are more narrow in their application.
   d. they mostly work with theories that have broader applications.

4. In an experiment the _____ variable is manipulated and the _____ variable is measured.
   a. dependent; independent
   b. confounding; dependent
   c. independent; dependent
   d. confounding; independent

5. You are studying the immediate effects of alcohol on people's feelings of well-being. Which of the following could be the dependent variable in this study?
   a. level of alcohol in the blood
   b. score on a measure of well-being
   c. amount of alcohol consumed within an hour prior to test
   d. either a or c

6. Understanding personality with an in-depth evaluation of a single individual or group of people is called
   a. the hypothesis-testing method.
   b. the experimental method.
   c. introspection.
   d. the case study method.

7. Among the psychologists who made use of the case study method in developing their ideas about personality was
   a. Sigmund Freud.
   b. Gordon Allport.
   c. Carl Rogers.
   d. all of the above

8. Among the disadvantages of the case study method is
   a. the possibility of bias.
   b. the difficulty with determining relationships among variables.
   c. the difficulty of examining certain concepts experimentally.
   d. the problem of illustrating a treatment.

9. Which of the following is a statistical test of significance used by personality researchers?
   a. analysis of variance
   b. chi-square test
   c. correlation coefficient
   d. all of the above

10. Herman wants to determine if there is a relationship between the penalty for not wearing seat belts and the number of accident-related deaths in certain states. Which of the following would be the most appropriate statistical test?
    a. chi-square
    b. correlation coefficient
    c. analysis of variance
    d. all of the above

11. Which of the following describes the relationship between your checking account balance and the amount of money you withdraw on several occasions?
    a. a perfect negative correlation
    b. a weak negative correlation
    c. a perfect positive correlation
    d. a strong positive correlation

12. Which of the following is the strongest correlation coefficient?
    a. 0.89
    b. - 0.98
    c. 0.00
    d. - 0.01

13. Which of the following is *not* a problem investigators face when designing their studies?
    a. making sure the independent variable does not vary with another variable
    b. developing a hypothesis before the results of a study are obtained
    c. relying on one research finding as evidence for the strength of an effect
    d. providing a comparison group in which subjects do not receive the experimental treatment.

14. In a study of the effects of uncontrollable noise on learned helplessness, the researcher randomly assigns participants to three different noise levels: high, moderate, and low. Assuming that the researcher eliminated the possibility that other variables besides noise may vary with the treatment conditions, what problem still remains?
    a. experimental confounds
    b. the use of a comparison group
    c. the problem of prediction versus hindsight
    d. difficulty replicating the study

15. Which of the following is true about replication in experimental research?
    a. We often use different experimental methods to reach different conclusions.
    b. We deal with the problem of prediction versus hindsight by replicating the results of original research.
    c. We often use participant populations different from those used in original research.
    d. We tend to explain effects after the data are in.

16. Which of the following is a problem of reliability?
    a. test responses are dependent on recent events
    b. test responses gauge the test takers' level on a hypothetical construct dimension
    c. test responses are judged subjectively
    d. none of the above

17. Which of the following is a problem of validity?
    a. test questions are vague
    b. test responses are dependent on recent events
    c. test responses do not reflect the hypothetical construct of interest
    d. none of the above

18. Which of the following test-retest coefficients is the most acceptable?
    a. .35
    b. .80
    c. .22
    d. -.90

19. Hypothetical constructs
    a. are actual events in the lives of individuals.
    b. explain the structure of hypotheses.
    c. are useful inventions used to describe concepts.
    d. are dependent on one's intelligence.

20. By looking at the items of a test researchers can determine the test's
    a. construct validity.
    b. face validity.
    c. discriminant validity.
    d. behavioral validity.

21. When scores from a test correlate with other measures of the same construct researcher's can determine the test's
    a. congruent validity.
    b. face validity.
    c. construct validity.
    d. discriminant validity.

Answers to Multiple Choice Questions

1.	c, 21	8.	a, 30	15.	c, 38
2.	b, 21	9.	d, 32	16.	a, 40
3.	c, 22	10.	b, 34	17.	c, 40
4.	c, 24	11.	a, 34	18.	b, 39
5.	b, 25	12.	b, 34	19.	c, 40
6.	d, 29	13.	b, 34	20.	b, 41
7.	d, 29	14.	b, 36	21.	a, 41

Integrative Questions

1. Review what Ann Landers wrote to "Desperate in Dallas," "Wondering in Boston," and "Intrigued in Norfolk" in the first paragraph of the chapter in the text. If you were to address the questions put to Ann with empirical research, then what would be the hypothesis to be tested in each of these cases? What variables would be considered in each? What results would be expected if Ann were correct in her answers?

2. Develop a hypothesis of your own about why some students study more than others. Identify the independent and dependent variables in your hypothesis and briefly describe an experiment to test your hypothesis. What is the "outcome" variable?

3. Contrast the experimental method and the case study method as means of understanding personality. What are the goals of each? How do they differ? What kind of data is collected in each?

4. Develop a sketch of a study of your own in which the correlation coefficient is the appropriate statistical test. From your example study, describe three possible outcomes of the test and what each outcome indicates about the variables in your study. Give values for the correlation coefficient that reflect these three different outcomes.

5. Suppose you wanted to investigate whether viewing violence on television causes children to be more aggressive. Describe your own experimental method to address this question. Illustrate how you would handle the problems of experimental confounds, comparison groups, and hindsight in your example.

6. Discuss the concepts of test-retest reliability and internal consistency, contrasting the difference in their meaning and the way in which each concept is measured and indexed.

7. Give an example of a personality test that has high construct but low face validity. What does discriminative validity tell you about a test measure?

Evaluative Questions

1. What makes a theory good? Briefly evaluate each of the six general approaches to personality that you learned about in Chapter 1 with respect to the characteristics of good theories.

2. Why do you think it was stated in the text that theories are never proven or disproven? State the advantages and disadvantages to testing hypotheses without a larger theory underlying them. In what research context is atheoretical research meaningful?

3. Suppose a researcher came to the following conclusion from a study: "The severity of a patient's psychosis makes them more or less able to seek treatment." From what you know about manipulated versus nonmanipulated independent variables, do you have any concerns about this conclusion? If so, specify the problem.

4. Can we come to understand personality using the case study method alone? Does the method have a place in personality research? Justify.

5. Can researchers ever tell if the different averages for their groups represent real effects of independent variables?

6. The author states that there is no such thing as a perfect experiment. In your own words, give the author's reasoning for making this statement. Do you agree or disagree? What is the solution to the imperfect nature of research? Support your answer.

7. Sigmund Freud made careful observations of his neurotic patients and from his notes he formulated the basis of his psychoanalytic theory. Then Freud applied his theoretical concepts to everyday psychology and attempted to explain everything about the personality. From a modern scientist's perspective, which of the problems to look for when examining research did Freud fail to look for? What are the implications of this problem for Freud's theory?

8. When we consider the reliability and the validity of a personality test, why is the question *not* whether the test has either of these characteristics or not? Explain whether it is possible for a test to have face validity, congruent validity, and discriminant validity and still have questionable construct validity.

Chapter **3**

The Psychoanalytic Approach
Freudian Theory, Application, and Assessment

Chapter Outline

Freud Discovers the Unconscious
The Freudian Theory of Personality
    The Topographic Model
    The Structural Model
    Instincts and Tension Reduction
    Defense Mechanisms
        Repression
        Sublimation
        Displacement
        Denial
        Reaction Formation
        Intellectualization
        Projection
    Psychosexual Stages of Development
    Getting at Unconscious Material
        Dreams
        Projective Tests
        Free Association
        Freudian Slips
        Hypnosis
        "Accidents"
        Symbolic Behavior
Application: Psychoanalysis
Assessment: Projective Tests
    Types of Projective Tests
    Evaluation of Projective Tests
Strengths and Criticisms of Freud's Theory

Learning Objectives

1. Give three examples of ways in which Freudian theory has influenced our culture.
2. Tell the story of how Freud discovered the unconscious in your own words.
3. Describe the topographic model proposed by Freud. State the divisions of the human personality in the topographic model and give an example of material from each.
4. Describe the structural model of personality proposed by Freud. Explain where in the topographic model can be found each of the three parts of the structural model.
5. Define id, ego, and superego. State the objective of each structure and the principles on which each rests.
6. Give the name and meaning behind each of the two major categories of instinct. Explain how psychic energy and each of these drives are involved in psychological functions.
7. List by name each of the Freudian ego defense mechanisms and give a definition and example for each. Identify the most and least successful defense mechanisms.
8. Describe each of the stages of psychosexual development. State the tenets upon which Freud's theory of personality development rests. For each stage give the approximate ages and an example of a fixation.
9. Describe each of the various techniques for getting at unconscious material. Specify the importance and function of dreams according to Freud. State the ways in which the unconscious is revealed in everyday life.
10. Discuss Freud's system of psychotherapy to treat psychological disorders. Explain the basis of psychoanalysis and describe the techniques used to get at crucial unconscious material and how the material is interpreted.
11. Explain the role of resistance and the roles of transference and countertransference in the therapy process. State the optimal outcome of successful treatment.
12. Discuss the use of projective tests as a means of assessment in psychoanalysis. Give the names and a description of three projective tests. State the criticisms that have been made and potential misuses of projective tests.
13. Give the strengths of the psychoanalytic approach to personality. State the benefits for which we can give Freud credit and discuss Freud's place in history.
14. State three general criticisms that can be made of Freud's theory of personality. Explain why some argue that Freud's ideas do not make a valuable scientific theory.

Important Concepts

hysteria (p. 46)
topographic model (p. 49)
structural model (p. 50)
id (p. 50)
wish fulfillment (p. 50)
ego (p. 50)
superego (p. 51)
anxiety (p. 53)
defense mechanisms (p. 53)
denial (p. 56)
reaction formation (p. 56)
oral stage (p. 58)
anal stage (p. 58)
phallic stage (p. 59)
Oedipus complex (p. 59)
latency stage (p. 59)
genital stage (p. 59)
free association (p. 62)
Freudian slips (p. 62)
psychoanalysis (p. 64)
Rorschach inkblot test (p. 67)
Thematic Apperception Test (p. 68)
Human Figure Drawing test (p. 68)

conscious (p. 49)
preconscious (p. 49)
unconscious (p. 50)
pleasure principle (p. 50)
reality principle (p. 50)
libido (p. 52)
Thanatos (p. 52)
repression (p. 53)
sublimation (p. 55)
displacement (p. 56)
intellectualization (p. 56)
projection (p. 57)
fixation (p. 57)
erogenous zone (p. 57)
castration anxiety (p. 59)
penis envy (p. 59)
manifest content (p. 61)
latent content (p. 61)
projective tests (p. 61)
resistance (p. 66)
transference (p. 66)
countertransference (p. 66)

Programmed Review

Most people in this culture freely accept the idea that behavior is sometimes influenced by an _____ part of the mind.

unconscious   p. 46

People who suffer from _____ display a variety of symptoms such as blindness, the inability to use an arm, or the loss of language.

hysteria   p. 46

Three parts of the personality the differ in terms of level of awareness make up the _____ model in Freudian theory.

topographic   p. 49

Freud described the conscious and preconscious as merely the tip of the _____ .

iceberg   p. 50

Actions taken by the id are based on the _____ principle.

pleasure   p. 50

The primary job of the _____ is to satisfy id impulses in a manner that takes into consideration reality.

ego   p. 50

People who suffer from an ever-present feeling of shame or guilt suffer from _____ .

moral anxiety   p. 52

The life instinct or sexual drive to which Freud attributed most behavior is called the _____ .

libido   p. 52

The techniques the ego uses to deal with unwanted thoughts and desires are collectively known as _____ .

defense mechanisms   p. 53

According to Freud, the defense mechanism upon which the whole structure of psychoanalysis rests is _____ .

repression   p. 53

More than just saying we don't remember, as in repression, _____ is a defense mechanism in which we simply refuse to accept the facts.

denial   p. 56

Removing the emotional content from an unwanted or threatening thought is known as _____ .

intellectualization   p. 56

The roots of adult personality are formed in the early years of life during the _____ stages of development.

psychosexual   p. 57

The first stage of personality development each child goes through is the _____ .

oral stage   p. 58

Boys develop _____ when they fear that their father will discover their incestuous desires for their mother.

castration anxiety   p. 59

The time before puberty is a time when sexual desires abate, called the _____ .

latency stage   p. 59

According to Freud, _____ are the "royal road to the unconscious" and represent the things and events we desire.

dreams   p. 60

Misstatements that reveal underlying unconscious feelings are called _____ .

Freudian slips   p. 62

According to Freud, many of our daily behaviors are _____ gestures of unconscious desires and thoughts.

symbolic   p. 63

Freud's system of psychotherapy is known as _____ .

psychoanalysis   p. 64

When patients declare to their therapist that the therapy isn't helping and they want to stop, the patient is developing a necessary part of therapy called _____ .

resistance   p. 66

Freud cautioned against _____ in which therapists displace their own feelings toward other people onto the patient.

countertransference   p. 66

When a therapist presents a patient with ambiguous stimuli, he or she is using a _____ .

projective test   p. 66

Multiple Choice Questions

1. Which of the following is an example of an everyday concept that comes from Freud?
    a. denial
    b. libido
    c. repression
    d. all of the above

2. The neurologist in Paris who demonstrated hypnosis to Freud was
    a. Breuer
    b. Charcot
    c. Jung
    d. Jones

3. Which of the following is true about hypnosis?
    a. Freud never used hypnosis to treat his patients' symptoms.
    b. After using hypnosis for a time, Freud began using it exclusively.
    c. Hypnosis is not a real phenomenon because people cannot really be hypnotized.
    d. Freud grew disillusioned by hypnosis and started using free association.

4. Which of the following is true about Freud's early work?
    a. He enjoyed complete acceptance from his professional colleagues from the start.
    b. After some initial success, Freud's techniques failed to work and his reputation soon suffered.
    c. Freud never spoke of his views of infantile sexuality because he feared opposition.
    d. His work was opposed by the academic and medical communities.

5. Memories of past events and other information that is easily retrievable comprise the
    a. conscious.
    b. preconscious.
    c. unconscious.
    d. structural model.

6. The id, ego, and superego are three parts of the _____ model of personality.
    a. topographic
    b. iceberg
    c. structural
    d. unconscious

7. The actions of the ego follow the _____ principle.
   a. pleasure
   b. reality
   c. morality
   d. ethical

8. If the superego could talk, which of the following would it most probably say?
   a. "I am so mad that I could bash in that person's skull."
   b. "Why not tell the person to respect the privacy of others."
   c. "Now you know you don't hate anyone."
   d. "I want to have sex with that person right now."

9. Lisa is a married woman who sees her doctor whenever she has the slightest symptom of a physical problem because she is attracted to him. It is most probably her _____ that decides to behave this way.
   a. id
   b. ego
   c. superego
   d. superid

10. In his thinking about the sexual instinct, Freud
    a. meant only those sexually motivated behaviors that result in intercourse.
    b. was referring to the life force that leads ultimately to death.
    c. included any actions initiated by the id that are aimed at receiving pleasure.
    d. proposed that it is limited such that the human race will be extinct eventually.

11. When we see our own unwanted thoughts and undesirable impulses in other people we are using the defense mechanism called _____ .
    a. projection
    b. reaction formation
    c. intellectualization
    d. displacement

12. One way to think of the concept of fixation is that fixation occurs during development when
    a. children leave behind some psychic energy tied up in resolving a crisis.
    b. we use defense mechanisms to deal with unconscious impulses.
    c. the rewards in the environment control our behaviors.
    d. all of the above

13. The Oedipus complex is part of the _____ stage of psychosexual development.
    a. oral
    b. anal
    c. phallic
    d. genital

14. George chews on his fingernails when he is nervous. Sometimes he chews gum. George is most likely fixated at which psychosexual stage of development?
    a. oral
    b. anal
    c. phallic
    d. genital

15. Which of the following techniques for getting at unconscious material was characterized by Freud as a type of wish fulfillment?
    a. free association
    b. Freudian slips
    c. symbolic behavior
    d. dreams

16. The use of _____ requires an individual to respond to ambiguous stimuli.
    a. free association
    b. dream analysis
    c. hypnosis
    d. projective tests

17. If a patient receiving psychoanalysis displaces emotions for other people on the therapist, then which of the following has taken place?
    a. wish fulfillment
    b. resistance
    c. transference
    d. countertransference

18. Sally is undergoing psychoanalysis for the treatment of her psychological problems. She is give a set of cards on which ambiguous pictures of people are displayed. Sally therapist is using the
    a. Rorschach inkblot test.
    b. Thematic Apperception Test.
    c. Free Association test.
    d. Human Figure Drawing test.

Answers to Multiple Choice Questions

1.	d, 46	7.	b, 50	13.	c, 59
2.	b, 46	8.	c, 51	14.	a, 58
3.	d, 48	9.	b, 51	15.	d, 60
4.	d, 49	10.	c, 52	16.	d, 61
5.	b, 49	11.	a, 57	17.	c, 66
6.	c, 50	12.	a, 57	18.	b, 68

Integrative Questions

1. Tell the story of how Freud discovered the unconscious in your own words. Include in the story examples of hysteria and the use of hypnosis and free association.

2. Describe the component structures in Freud's structural model. Explain where each structure fits within the topographic model. State the kinds of anxiety that result from lack of control of each of the three structures of personality.

3. Make a list of the defense mechanisms proposed by Freud. For each mechanism give an example from your own life or someone you know that has used the defense mechanism to reduce or avoid anxiety.

4. State the similarities and differences between each of the following pairs of defense mechanisms:
    (a) repression and denial
    (b) sublimation and displacement
    (c) reaction formation and projection

5. Describe each of the stages of psychosexual development in order, giving the approximate age which each stage takes place and an example of a fixation at each stage. Choose one fixation and give an example of adult behavior that results from it.

6. State how the process of free association, taking projective tests and making Freudian slips are alike. In other words, what is the fundamental idea behind each of these as ways of getting at unconscious material?

7. Describe the series of events in a typical course of treatment using psychoanalysis. What must take place for the patient's treatment to be considered a success?

8. Discuss and compare the three types of projective tests described in the text. Under what circumstances would one type of test be used rather than another?

Evaluative Questions

1. Why is it said that Freud's approach to treating psychological disorders was radical? Why was it not accepted by other physicians of his day? Given what you know about personality research methods from Chapter 2, evaluate Freud's theory and methods of assessment. In other words, if Freud's approach was new today would it be any more accepted than it was then?

2. There have been many approaches to mental functioning and models of mental structure in the past 100 years in psychology. Why do you suppose Freud thought of the mind as forces pulling and pushing at one another? Do you agree with this conceptualization of the mind and structure of personality? Why or why not?

3. What do you think of Freud's statement that dreams are the "royal road to the unconscious"? Give evidence from your own dreams to explain why you agree or disagree. Evaluate Freud's dream theory in terms of the validity of the interpretation of symbolic representations in dreams.

4. Of all the various ways to get at the unconscious, with which do you think the most material can be uncovered? Support your answer and state how the psychoanalyst uses the technique.

5. State the ultimate goal of psychoanalysis. How does the therapist know treatment has been a success? How does the outcome of treatment fit Freud's overall approach to personality?

6. Summarize point by point the evaluation of projective tests given in the textbook. With which points do you agree and with which do you disagree? Clearly state your reasoning.

7. Given what you know about Freud's life history, what aspects of his approach to personality reflect his experience and the times in which he lived? If Freud had been a women, all other things being equal, discuss how you think his approach to personality would have been different.

Chapter **4**

The Freudian Approach: Relevant Research

Chapter Outline

Dream Interpretation
    The Meaning of Dream Content
    The Function of Dreams
The Oedipus Complex
    Subliminal Psychodynamic Activation
    Research on the Oedipus Complex
    Criticisms and Challenges
Humor
    Freud's Theory of Humor
    Research on Freud's Theory of Humor
        Preference for Hostile Humor
        Reducing Aggression with Hostile Humor
        Level of Tension and Funniness
        Interpreting the Research Findings
Hypnosis
    What Is Hypnosis?
        Psychoanalytically Influenced Theories
    Socio-Cognitive Theories of Hypnosis
        Posthypnotic Amnesia
    Hypnotic Responsiveness

Learning Objectives

1. Summarize general criticisms of Freud's approach to personality. State some aspects of Freud's theory that have been examined by research.

2. State why Freud examined and interpreted his patients' dreams. Discuss the kinds of contents dreams contain and Freud's explanation of the recurrent dream.

3. Discuss Freud's response to the challenge of explaining why we dream. Specify the different kinds of sleep according to modern research. State the value of REM sleep and how it was determined. Give research evidence in support of Freud's dream theory.
4. Describe the Oedipus complex according to Freud. State the problems associated with conducting experiments on the Oedipus complex.
5. Describe the research of Silverman and colleagues on psychodynamic activation. Identify what is meant by the term "subliminal." Summarize the research evidence related to the Oedipus complex using subliminal psychodynamic activation.
6. Discuss the criticisms and challenges facing research aimed at investigating the Oedipus complex. State several responses to the criticisms of subliminal psychodynamic activation research that support Freud's work.
7. State the significance of humor for Freud and discuss his theory of humor. Explain the relationship between humor and hostility and sex.
8. Summarize the research findings on Freud's theory of humor. Specify the predictions made by Freudian theory with respect to humor and whether these predictions are supported by the relevant research.
9. Define hypnosis. Give a description of hypnotic induction and responsiveness.
10. Describe the approach to hypnosis known as neodissociation theory. State the research evidence in support of this theory.
11. Describe the socio-cognitive approach to hypnosis. State the research evidence in support of this approach.
12. Define posthypnotic amnesia and hypnotic responsiveness. Describe the psychoanalytic explanations for these phenomena and give one argument against the Freudian approach for each.
13. Summarize the characteristics of a person who is responsive to hypnosis. Define absorption and describe its relationship to hypnotic responsiveness. State the three variables that affect hypnotic responsiveness.

Important Concepts

symbolism (p. 80)
electroencephalograph (p. 83)
tachistoscope (p. 85)
hostile humor (p. 91)
hypnosis (p. 95)
posthypnotic amnesia (p. 98)
hypnotic responsiveness (p. 99)

paradoxical sleep (p. 83)
REM sleep (p. 83)
subliminal psychodynamic activation (p. 85)
"tendentious" jokes (p. 89)
neodissociation theory (p. 97)
socio-cognitive theory (p. 97)
absorption (p. 101)

Programmed Review

Freud sought validation of his theory through _____ rather than empirical experiments.

case study reports   p. 78

According to Freud, the content of our dreams contains much information about what's in our _____ .

unconscious   p. 80

In dreams important unconscious material has been disguised through _____ .

symbolism   p. 80

REM sleep is sometimes called _____ sleep.

paradoxical   p. 83

One result of the Oedipus complex is that men seek a _____ with their mothers.

symbolic relationship   p. 84

In the research on subliminal psychodynamic activation, images are flashes on a screen by a device called a _____ .

tachistoscope   p. 85

Freud was not concerned with puns and clever insights, rather he was concerned with what he called _____ jokes.

"tendentious"   p. 89

According to Freud, jokes like those that attack marriage or other institutions often have disguised _____ .

hostility   p. 90

While often misunderstood, hypnosis carries a number of potentially useful _____ .

applications   p. 95

According to one explanation of hypnosis, the _____ forms a new subsystem when a person is under hypnosis.

ego   p. 97

Hypnosis researchers have asked participants to report their experience through "automatic writing," that is taken as evidence for a _____ observer that is aware of what's going on.

hidden   p. 97

When hypnosis participants are told they will not remember what has happened during hypnosis, the hypnotist is inducing _____ .

posthypnotic amnesia   p. 98

People who score high on measures of _____ are more responsive to hypnotic suggestions.

absorption   p. 101

Multiple Choice Questions

1. A scientific approach to personality requires
    a. more than faith in one theory over another.
    b. that theory fit our personal perceptions.
    c. some understanding of our own feelings and behaviors.
    d. keen insight.

2. Freud interpreted his patients' dreams as a means of
    a. understanding their conscious awareness.
    b. developing different theories of personality.
    c. understanding their unconscious conflicts and desires.
    d. clever hypnotic suggestion.

3. Which is true about the characters in men's dreams?
    a. The number of male characters is equal to the number of female characters.
    b. The number of male and female characters is equal to the number in women's dreams.
    c. Men are more likely to dream about female characters than male characters.
    d. Men are more likely to dream about male characters than female characters.

4. According to the research findings, recurrent dreamers are likely to
   a. suffer from a failure to control aggressive behavior.
   b. be well adjusted during waking hours.
   c. suffer from anxiety and generally poor adjustment during waking hours.
   d. be high achievers who display a high level of self confidence.

5. Dreams take place during a kind of sleep called
   a. REM sleep.
   b. paradoxical sleep.
   c. non-REM sleep.
   d. both a and b

6. According to recent research findings, REM sleep appears to be necessary to
   a. maintain one's mental health.
   b. guard against serious psychological disturbances.
   c. prepare us for dealing with anxiety-arousing events.
   d. all of the above

7. Which of the following is an assumption of the subliminal psychodynamic activation procedure?
   a. The information presented to participants is retained in consciousness.
   b. Flashing images on a screen can induce immediate REM sleep.
   c. The unconscious can register images presented for only a fraction of a second.
   d. Any kind of psychological disturbance can be treated successfully with it.

8. Which is a result of research using the subliminal psychodynamic activation procedure?
   a. Depressed people presented with aggressive images became more depressed.
   b. Orally dependent personalities showed a strong physiological reaction to messages like "No one loves me."
   c. People who stutter increased their stuttering when presented with images of a dog defecating.
   d. all of the above

9. Men who played darts before and after exposure to subliminal messages performed better when the message was
   a. Beating Dad Is Wrong.
   b. People Are Walking.
   c. Beating Dad Is OK.
   d. Mommy and I Are One.

10. The most serious reservation about subliminal psychodynamic activation research is that
    a. results have been difficult to replicate.
    b. the validity of the interpretation has been questioned.
    c. the use of messages has proved less adequate than the presentation of images.
    d. the studies have not included that proper controls.

11. Which of the following is *false* about sexual jokes?
    a. Jokes are often tolerated when open discussions of sex are inappropriate.
    b. Most sexually oriented jokes contain a great deal of humor.
    c. Freud suggested we laugh at sexual jokes to reduce tension.
    d. Freud argued that the humor content of a sexual joke rarely justifies the laughter.

12. When researchers asked high school students to write funny captions to pictures,
    a. more young men responded with sexual captions than young women.
    b. the students gave a great deal of responses with aggressive and sexual themes.
    c. the word "mother" was used in the majority of responses.
    d. responses that suggested pain or violence were nearly completely absent.

13. With respect to humor and tension reduction, Freud suggested that a joke will be funnier
    a. when it is sexual than when it is hostile.
    b. the less tension that is experienced before the punch line.
    c. when tension increases rapidly.
    d. the more tension that is experienced before the punch line.

14. The view that deeply hypnotized people experience a division of their consciousness is known as
    a. neodissociation theory.
    b. socio-cognitive theory.
    c. trance theory.
    d. neonatal theory.

15. When researchers told participants under hypnosis that their "hidden observer" would experience less pain, then the participants reported
    a. more pain.
    b. less pain.
    c. no change in pain.
    d. a loss of hypnotic responsiveness.

16. One method used to break through posthypnotic amnesia was
    a. Telling participants that a lie detector indicates they were lying.
    b. Showing participants a videotape of their hypnotic experience.
    c. Encouraging participants to be honest.
    d. all of the above

17. In which of the following circumstances are people more responsive to hypnosis?
    a. when the situation is not defined as hypnosis
    b. when the participant has not been responsive to hypnosis in the past
    c. when the cooperation and trust of the participant is established
    d. both a and b

18. Which of the following majors probably has the greatest percentage of students who are responsive to hypnotic suggestion?
    a. biology major
    b. theater major
    c. nursing major
    d. philosophy major

19. Which of the following is *not* a variable that determines hypnotic responsiveness?
    a. motivation
    b. expectancy
    c. attitude
    d. intelligence

Answers to Multiple Choice Questions

1.	a, 78	11.	b, 90
2.	c, 80	12.	b, 90
3.	d, 81	13.	d, 93
4.	c, 82	14.	a, 97
5.	d, 83	15.	b, 98
6.	c, 83	16.	d, 99
7.	c, 85	17.	c, 100
8.	d, 85	18.	b, 101
9.	c, 87	19.	d, 102
10.	a, 88		

Integrative Questions

1. Summarize at least three general criticisms of Freud's approach to personality. What aspects of Freud's theory have been examined by research? Is all the research evidence in support of Freud's work? Explain.

2. What do people dream about? Why do people dream? Give a Freudian interpretation of the research findings on dreams in your answer to these questions.

3. Give a description of your own of the subliminal psychodynamic activation procedure and list the research evidence that supports the Oedipus complex. Of the criticisms of this research, which is the most serious and why?

4. Try a small study in which you pick three friends and ask each of them to write down their three favorite jokes. According to Freud's theory of humor and the relevant research, what do you expect to find in terms of the content of these nine jokes? After collecting the data, can you say that your expectation was confirmed? Speculate on the outcome of your study.

5. State three specific predictions of Freud's theory about aggressive humor. Summarize the evidence for a preference for hostile humor, the reduction of aggression with hostile humor, and the relationship between tension reduction and funniness. Give an alternative explanation for each of these predictions.

6. Describe the continuum on which theorists fall with respect to hypnosis. What are the extreme positions on the continuum? Where do you fall on the continuum and why?

7. According to socio-cognitive theories of hypnosis, what is the difference between hypnotized and nonhypnotized people who comply to a request? What criticisms have been made of the hidden observer demonstrations? Why have some argued that the psychoanalytic position on hypnosis is circular?

8. List the techniques used to breach posthypnotic amnesia. List the methods that have been shown to increase hypnotic responsiveness. Explain why hypnosis is largely a participant variable.

9. Is it possible to train people to be more responsive to hypnotic suggestions? Give an example of a study that demonstrated the researcher's ability to increase responsiveness.

Evaluative Questions

1. Consider an example from your own life of a feeling or behavior that is readily explained by psychoanalytic theory. Specifically describe the insight psychoanalysis provides in this respect. Contrast the readily explained feeling or behavior with another that is not easily explained by psychoanalytic theory.

2. Document a dream of your own that you remember from either the recent past or from childhood. Identify the symbols in the dream and give at least three different interpretations of your dream. Which interpretation appeals to you the most and why?

3. Summarize the research findings that challenge Freud's theory of dreaming. Given that human adults are not the only creatures that experience REM sleep, evaluate the claim made by Freud that dreams are wish fulfillments of the unconscious.

4. Given that Freud's approach to personality posits such a significant role for the unconscious in every aspect of our lives and its strong influence on our behaviors, what do you make of the difficulty to replicate even the most basic findings for unconscious activation in the laboratory? Should we not find strong evidence for the existence of the unconscious and large effects of its influence on behavior? Why or why not?

5. Describe the debate between the neodissociation view and the socio-cognitive view of hypnosis. Include the central issues and the explanations of hypnosis given by each of these approaches. With which do you agree and why?

6. Describe the personality of an individual who is highly responsive to hypnosis. What are the characteristics of the hypnotically responsive person? Give examples from your own life to illustrate whether you possess the characteristics of a person who is responsive to hypnosis.

Chapter **5**

The Psychoanalytic Approach: Neo-Freudian Theory, Application, and Assessment

Chapter Outline

Limits and Liabilities of Freudian Theory
Alfred Adler
    Striving for Superiority
    Parental Influence on Personality Development
    Birth Order
Carl Jung
    The Collective Unconscious
    Some Important Archetypes
    Evidence for the Collective Unconscious
Erik Erikson
    Erikson's Concept of the Ego
    Personality Development Throughout the Life Cycle
Karen Horney
    Neurosis
    Feminine Psychology
Harry Stack Sullivan
    Personifications
    Developmental Epochs
Erich Fromm
    Mechanisms of Escape
    Positive Freedom
Application: Psychoanalytic Theory and Religion
Assessment: Measuring Types
    Jung's Theory of Psychological Types
        Measuring Psychological Types: The Myers-Briggs Type Indicator
Strengths and Criticisms of Neo-Freudian Theories

Learning Objectives

1. State three limits and liabilities of Freudian theory.
2. Discuss Adler's contribution to psychoanalytic theory and identify the main points of his approach. State the role of inferiority for Adler and the basic factors that influence personality development.
3. Discuss Jung's contribution to psychoanalytic theory and identify the main points of his approach. Define collective unconscious and describe its contents. State the evidence Jung gave for the collective unconscious.
4. Discuss Erikson's contribution to psychoanalytic theory and identify the main points of his approach. Define identity crisis and describe Erikson's conception of the ego. List the basic stages of personality development according to Erikson and with each stage state the basic crisis involved.
5. Discuss Horney's contribution to psychoanalytic theory and identify the specific objections she had to Freud's original theory. Explain Horney's conception of neurosis and the three general social interaction styles neurotic people adopt.
6. Discuss Sullivan's contribution to psychoanalytic theory. Define personifications and describe the role of social interactions in his approach. List the developmental epochs according to Sullivan and give a characterization of each of the three epochs of adolescence.
7. Discuss Fromm's contribution to psychoanalytic theory and specify the logic behind his approach. Describe three strategies to escape freedom and the concept of positive freedom.
8. State Freud's view of religion and its role in human life. Contrast Freud's view with that of Jung and Fromm. State Jung's answer to the question of God's existence.
9. Compare the methods of assessment used by Neo-Freudian psychologists to that used by Freudian psychologists. Describe Jung's theory of psychological types and how it evolved.
10. Describe the Myers-Briggs Type Indicator and specify the contexts under which it is used for personality assessment. Explain the best ways in which the Myers-Briggs Type Indicator can be applied to education.
11. State the strengths of the neo-Freudian theories of personality. Identify the ways in which neo-Freudian approaches have influenced later theorists.
12. State two general criticisms that can be made of neo-Freudian theories of personality.

Important Concepts

neo-Freudians (p. 106)
individual psychology (p. 107)
striving for superiority (p. 108)
inferiority complex (p. 108)

analytic psychology (p. 112)
collective unconscious (p. 114)
primordial images (p. 114)
archetypes (p. 114)
ego psychology (p. 119)
neurosis (p. 127)
externalization (p. 129)
womb envy (p. 130)
personification (p. 132)
developmental epochs (p. 133)
positive freedom (p. 139)
authoritarianism (p. 135)
authoritarian religions (p. 141)
humanistic religions (p. 141)

birth order (p. 110)
personal unconscious (p. 114)
anima/animus (p. 115)
shadow (p. 116)
identity crisis (p. 119)
moving toward people (p. 128)
moving against people (p. 129)
moving away from people (p. 129)
selective inattention (p. 132)
automaton conformity (p. 138)
individuation (p. 138)
psychological type (p. 142)
introversion (p. 143)
extraversion (p. 143)

Programmed Review

Many theorists after Freud addressed the positive features of the ego and emphasized the role of the _____ .

conscious   p. 107

Alfred Adler called his approach _____ .

individual psychology   p. 107

According to Adler, two types of parental behavior sure to lead to personality problems are pampering and _____ .

neglect   p. 108

Jung believed that a part of the mind Freud neglected to talk about was the _____ .

collective unconscious   p. 114

The collective unconscious is made up of potentialities for responding called _____ .

primordial images (archetypes)   p. 114

The unconscious part of ourselves that is symbolized in the devil is known as _____ .

the shadow   p. 116

Erikson observed that overly protective parents hinder the development of a sense of _____ .

autonomy p. 121

According to Erikson, adults who fail to develop concern for the development of young people suffer from a sense of _____ .

stagnation p. 124

Horney said that _____ behavior starts with disturbed interpersonal relationships during childhood.

neurotic p. 127

Horney's concept of _____ is most similar to Freud's concept of projection.

externalization p. 129

The personification that reflects those parts of our experiences that we would rather not think about was called the _____ by Sullivan.

bad-me p. 132

Fromm suggested that people who show a combination of striving for submission and for domination are using the method of escape called _____ .

authoritarianism p. 135

Instead of escaping from freedom, Fromm suggested that we can choose to embrace it by the process of _____ .

individuation p. 138

Humanistic religions provide an opportunity for _____ .

personal growth p. 142

According to Jung, people who have an attitude of _____ have a dominant tendency to channel psychic energy inward.

introversion p. 143

According to Jung, sensation and feeling are the _____ functions.

irrational p. 143

Multiple Choice Questions

1. The neo-Freudian theories should be viewed as different perspectives within the general psychoanalytic approach because they retained the concept of
    a. the unconscious.
    b. defense mechanisms.
    c. dream interpretation.
    d. all of the above

2. Which of the following is *not* a key limitation to Freud's theory?
    a. the idea that the adult personality is formed by the time a child is five or six
    b. the idea that the ego defends against anxiety
    c. Freud's emphasis on instinctual influences on personality
    d. Freud's concentration on the negative parts of personality

3. Who was the first neo-Freudian theorist to break with Freud?
    a. Erik Erikson
    b. Karen Horney
    c. Carl Jung
    d. Alfred Adler

4. According to Adler, which of the following birth orders has the least number of personality problems?
    a. first-borns
    b. middle-borns
    c. last-borns
    d. only children

5. Which of the theorists named his approach *analytic psychology*?
    a. Alfred Adler
    b. Carl Jung
    c. Harry Stack Sullivan
    d. Erich Fromm

6. Which of the following is true about the collective unconscious?
    a. The collective unconscious consists of thoughts repressed out of consciousness.
    b. We acquire the collective unconscious from interactions with our parents.
    c. The collective unconscious is basically the same for all people.
    d. both a and c

7. Which of the following archetypes is the feminine side of the male?
    a. anima
    b. animus
    c. shadow
    d. light

8. According to Erikson, identity crises are more likely to occur when
   a. there is rapid social change.
   b. there is a threat of war.
   c. there is a social threat to personal values.
   d. any of the above

9. The approach to personality developed by Erik Erikson is known as
   a. analytic psychology.
   b. synthetic psychology.
   c. ego psychology.
   d. identity psychology.

10. Freud's anal stage of development is very similar to which of Erikson's stages?
    a. trust vs. mistrust
    b. autonomy vs. shame and doubt
    c. initiative vs. guilt
    d. industry vs. inferiority

11. According to Erikson, a person in middle adulthood is in the _____ stage of development.
    a. intimacy versus isolation
    b. generativity versus stagnation
    c. ego integrity versus despair
    d. industry versus inferiority

12. The general interaction style that Horney proposed for those who are extremely dependent on others is called
    a. moving toward people.
    b. moving against people.
    c. moving away from people.
    d. moving along with people.

13. According to Sullivan, one effective way to reduce the impact of anxiety-provoking information is to use
    a. dream interpretation.
    b. womb envy.
    c. selective inattention.
    d. neurotic strategies.

14. George is thinking about the A grade he received on his psychology exam and how his studying increased his grade from his usual performance. Sullivan would say that George's personification is the
    a. good-me.
    b. bad-me.
    c. not-me.
    d. silly-me.

15. The developmental epoch signaled by a sex drive and need for an intimate relationship is
    a. juvenile era.
    b. preadolescence.
    c. early adolescence.
    d. late adolescence.

16. Fromm centered his theory on a basic need to _____ the anxiety of freedom.
    a. defend against
    b. discover
    c. progress toward
    d. escape from

17. The neo-Freudian theorist who stimulated the most discussion about psychology and religion was
    a. Alfred Alder.
    b. Carl Jung.
    c. Karen Horney.
    d. Erich Fromm.

18. Which of the following statements can be attributed to Jung's view of religion?
    a. "Authoritarian religions emphasize that we are under the control of a powerful God."
    b. "Humanistic religions emphasize that there is no God."
    c. "Modern psychotherapy has taken on the role once reserved for the clergy."
    d. "The religions of mankind must be classes among the mass-delusions."

19. According to Jung's theory of psychological types, which of the four basic functions is not a rational function?
    a. thinking
    b. feeling
    c. sensation
    d. all of the above

20. At an art museum Laura considers the value of one work of art and says that the artist must have been depressed when he created it. Which of the following is most likely the dominant function for Laura?
    a. thinking
    b. intuition
    c. sensation
    d. feeling

21. In addition to the psychological types described by Jung, the Myers-Briggs Type Indicator measures
    a. whether one is open to new information.
    b. the sensing-intuitive categories.
    c. the judgment-perception categories.
    d. both a and c

Answers to Multiple Choice Questions

1.	d, 106	8.	d, 119	15.	c, 133
2.	b, 107	9.	c, 119	16.	d, 135
3.	d, 107	10.	a, 120	17.	b, 140
4.	b, 110	11.	b, 124	18.	c, 141
5.	b, 112	12.	a, 128	19.	c, 143
6.	c, 114	13.	c, 132	20.	d, 143
7.	a, 115	14.	a, 132	21.	d, 145

Integrative Questions

1. List and elaborate on the three general limits and liabilities to Freud's theory. From your reading of the chapter, give specific examples of how neo-Freudian theorists handled these problems with Freud's theory.

2. In what ways is the inferiority complex like the behavioral/learning approach's concept of learned helplessness? What is the motivating force in life, according to Adler? Does Alder's view suggest that mental health comes from achievement? Why or why not?

3. Discuss the influence of parenting style and birth order on the personality according to Adler. Give examples of adult personalities that result from the three birth order categories. Identify yourself in terms of birth order and evaluate Adler's approach from your personal introspection.

4. Describe each of the various archetypes proposed by Jung to be in the collective unconscious. In what ways is each reflected in our personalities and culture? What did Jung call the process of becoming what we're supposed to become?

5. Contrast Erikson's conception of the ego with Freud's. In what specific ways does Erikson depart from Freud with respect to the ego and personality development?

6. List each of the stages of development according Erikson, including an example of each crisis. Contrast Erikson's stages of development with Sullivan's developmental epochs. In what ways do these schemes overlap? What characteristics and ages of onset are different between these two approaches?

7. Define "womb envy."

8. Make a list of the names of the neo-Freudian theorists. Next to each name on the list write one fact that distinguishes the theorist or theory from all the others.

9. What were the major influences on Fromm that led to his psychoanalytic theory? Discuss his mechanisms of escape and illustrate each with your own example. What defense mechanisms would Freud say roughly match each of Fromm's strategies? Explain.

10. According to Fromm, what is the foremost component of spontaneity? Discuss a way in which Fromm's approach is similar to that of humanistic psychologists.

11. What was Jung main interest in religion? How did Jung answer the question of God's existence? Why, according to Jung, is there a similar entity to the Judeo-Christian God in all cultures of the world?

Evaluative Questions

1. Consider the manner in which Freud and those who disagreed with Freud were viewed by his admirers. Critically evaluate the scientific status of the contributions of the neo-Freudians who broke with Freud and elaborated his theory.

2. What are the differences between the instincts Freud proposed and what Jung meant by the collective unconscious? Did Jung think there was any difference?

3. What is the main difficulty of Jungian psychology? What evidence did Jung provide for the collective unconscious? Based on the standards of scientific research you learned about in Chapter 2, state to what degree you think Jung's evidence was scientific.

4. Consider each of the three strategies Horney proposed by which people handle anxiety. Think of someone you know for each of these strategies and give evidence to support your categorization of each person.

5. What was Horney's explanation for Freud's observations and theories about women? What fundamental aspect of her approach is underscored by her difference with Freud over feminine psychology?

6. Choose three neo-Freudian theorists and give a critical evaluation of each one's theory in three paragraphs. Then in the fourth paragraph give evidence for or against the validity of each theorist's approach in your life.

7. Categorize yourself according to the eight psychological types in Table 5.2 on page 144 of your text. Now examine Table 5.3. Identify the kind of career that would be appropriate for your psychological type. Do the same for a friend and see if they agree with your analysis.

Chapter **6**

The Neo-Freudian Theories: Relevant Research

Chapter Outline

Anxiety and Coping Strategies
    Coping with Anxiety
    Active versus Avoidance Strategies
    Problem-Focused versus Emotion-Focused Strategies
    How Effective are Coping Strategies?
Frustration and Aggression
    The Frustration-Aggression Hypothesis
    Testing the Frustration-Aggression Hypothesis
        Does Frustration Always Lead to Aggression?
        Does Aggression Lead to Catharsis and Reduced Aggression?
    A Revised Frustration-Aggression Hypothesis
Attachment Style and Adult Relationships
    Object Relations Theory and Attachment Theory
    Adult Attachment Styles
    Attachment Style and Romantic Relationships
    An Alternate Model of Adult Attachment Style

Learning Objectives

1. Identify three types of anxiety according to Freud. State the purpose of coping strategies as seen by neo-Freudian theorists and what neo-Freudians meant by "defense mechanisms."

2. Distinguish coping strategies that are active from those that are avoidant and distinguish coping strategies that are problem-focused from emotion-focused strategies. State the relative effectiveness of these different strategies.

3. Explain the connection between frustration and aggression according to Freud.

4. State the frustration-aggression hypothesis and its several implications. Define catharsis and give its role in aggressive behavior.

5. Summarize the research findings from tests of the frustration-aggression hypothesis. State whether frustration always leads to aggression and whether reduced aggression is the result of aggression.

6. State the revised frustration-aggression hypothesis proposed by Berkowitz. List the advantages of this revision over the original hypothesis.

7. Explain why understanding adult romantic relationships begins with looking at very early childhood experiences. Discuss object relations theory and attachment theory. Specify three types of parent-child relationships and give an example of each.

8. Describe three adult attachment styles and state how each relate to happiness in romantic relationships. Give examples of the kind of interactions partners have within each attachment style.

9. Describe the distinctions among early attachment experiences that are made in an alternate model of adult attachment styles. Specify four categories of personalities with respect to attachment style.

Important Concepts

reality anxiety (p. 153)
neurotic anxiety (p. 153)
moral anxiety (p. 153)
frustration-aggression hypothesis (p. 162)
catharsis (p. 163)
indirect aggression (p. 164)
object relations theory (p. 172)
secure attachment style (p. 174)
avoidant attachment style (p. 174)

coping strategies (p. 155)
active-cognitive strategies (p. 157)
active-behavioral strategies (p. 157)
avoidance strategies (p. 157)
problem-focused strategies (p. 157)
emotion-focused strategies (p. 157)
coping style (p. 156)
anxious-ambivalent attachment style (p. 174)
four-category model of attachment style (p. 177)

Programmed Review

When you experience _____, you have feelings of worry, panic, and fear.

anxiety   p. 153

According to Horney, children faced with excessive anxiety develop styles of _____ that temporarily reduce anxiety.

interacting with others   p. 154

We refer to a person's general approach to dealing with stress as their _____ .

coping style   p. 156

People who actively think about a stressful situation to try to make things better use the _____ strategy.

active-cognitive   p. 157

_____ strategies are designed to reduce the emotional distress that accompanies problems.

Emotion-focused   p. 157

Some research has found the problem-focused strategies are more effective than emotion-focused strategies in helping people avoid _____ .

depression   p. 161

Freud suggested that when the libido is frustrated we experience a _____ of aggressing against the obstacle.

primordial reaction   p. 162

To explain when aggression will stop, researchers adopted the Freudian concept of _____ .

catharsis   p. 163

One reason why aggression breads aggression is because acting aggressively may lead to a _____ to aggress in the future.

disinhibition   p. 168

Berkowitz argues that frustrations cause us to act aggressively because they are _____ .

aversive   p. 169

The emotional attachment between infants and their care givers is called _____ .

attachment relationships   p. 172

A person who describes their relationships with family members as distrustful and emotionally distant most probably has a _____ style of attachment.

avoidant   p. 174

In terms of the four-category model of adult attachment, _____ people have feelings that they are unworthy while they tend to see others as trustworthy.

preoccupied											p. 177

Multiple Choice Questions

1. Harold feels anxious whenever the cheerleaders at school walk close by. When some girls speak to him, Harold turns red and often cannot speak. Which form of anxiety is Harold most likely experiencing?
    a. reality anxiety
    b. neurotic anxiety
    c. moral anxiety
    d. superego anxiety

2. In one study when participants were shown a film on industrial safety, the most common strategy for reducing the anxiety produced by the film was
    a. focusing on technical aspects of the film rather than the discomfort of the content.
    b. intellectualization.
    c. to remind themselves that what they were watching was only a film.
    d. both b and c

3. Along the *repression-sensitization* dimension, repressors
    a. try to think about a threatening situation in a rational way.
    b. try to avoid threatening situations.
    c. find out as much as possible about the stressful situation.
    d. used active-cognitive coping strategies.

4. With respect to gender differences in coping strategies,
    a. women use emotion-focused strategies more than men.
    b. men use emotion-focused strategies more than women.
    c. women take steps to solve problems directly more than men.
    d. none of the above

5. Which of the following is true about the effectiveness of coping strategies?
    a. The more people rely on coping strategies, the more anxiety they feel.
    b. Active strategies are more effective than avoidant strategies.
    c. The use of a coping strategy is more effective in reducing anxiety than not using one.
    d. Avoidance strategies are generally more effective in the long-run.

6. When investigators examined the coping strategies of Israeli soldiers who had suffered combat stress, which of the following was found to be most successful?
   a. problem-focused strategies
   b. emotion-focused strategies
   c. either problem-focused or emotion focused strategies
   d. only avoidant strategies

7. Which of the following is the name Freud gave to the death instinct?
   a. The Shadow
   b. libido
   c. Thanatos
   d. catharsis

8. With regard to the frustration-aggression hypothesis,
   a. most researchers today accept that aggression is always caused by frustration.
   b. it has been shown that aggression is always reduced by catharsis.
   c. frustration always leads to aggressive behavior.
   d. most researchers today accept that aggression can have a number of causes.

9. Which of the following is true about the frustration-aggression effect?
   a. Frustrated people act more aggressively than nonfrustrated people.
   b. Frustration is one cause of aggression.
   c. Aggressive responses are more likely when a frustrated person is close to their goal.
   d. all of the above

10. When angry participants in a study were allowed to retaliate against someone who frustrated them,
    a. the participants' blood pressure went up.
    b. greater aggression was shown after the participants experienced a release of tension.
    c. greater aggression was shown when there was no opportunity for cathartic release.
    d. acting aggressively lead to inhibition of further aggression.

11. In contrast to Freud's theory, object relations theorists
    a. focus on internal drives and conflicts.
    b. are interested in the intellectual and emotional development of the infant.
    c. do not believe that children develop unconscious representations of significant objects in their environment.
    d. are interested in an infant's relationship with its parents.

12. Which of the following statements would be most likely said by a person with an anxious-ambivalent style?
    a. "I'm uncomfortable around other people."
    b. "It is easy for me to get close to people."
    c. "I'm worried that my partner doesn't really love me."
    d. "Lovers often want to get more intimate with me than I want."

13. In a newspaper survey, secure adults reported that they had been in their current relationship
    a. for more than ten years.
    b. for less than six years.
    c. since puberty.
    d. for more than thirty years.

14. Which of the following categories of adult attachment is characterized by fear of being hurt?
    a. secure
    b. preoccupied
    c. dismissing
    d. fearful

Answers to Multiple Choice Questions

1. b, 153
2. c, 155
3. b, 156
4. a, 159
5. c, 159
6. a, 161
7. c, 162
8. d, 164
9. d, 164
10. b, 168
11. d, 172
12. c, 174
13. a, 176
14. c, 177

Integrative Questions

1. Contrast the strategies proposed by the neo-Freudian theorists that people use to reduce anxiety with the defense mechanisms Freud proposed. What is the essential difference between Freudian and neo-Freudian perspectives?

2. State the early version of the distinction between active and avoidant copy strategies. Give examples of a person's response to stress from each end of the dimension.

3. Which are the most effective coping strategies for reducing anxiety? From the evidence given in your textbook, give your best answer and support it.

4. Discuss how Freud's view of the relationship between frustration and aggression influenced research by behavioral psychologists on the topic. In what ways do the Freudian and behavioral approaches differ with respect to frustration-aggression? In what way is the revised frustration-aggression hypothesis even more behavioral in approach?

5. Describe three kinds of parent-child relationships. What are the implications for children in each of these relationships when they are adults? What will their romantic relationships probably be like?

6. Contrast the four categories of attachment styles in the alternate model of adult attachment styles. What would a person's attachment style be like who has a negative model of self and a positive model of others? What about a person who has a positive model of self and a negative model of others?

Evaluative Questions

1. Choose two examples of research from the chapter and identify the psychoanalytic concepts involved in the research. How did the neo-Freudians adapt each concept from Freud's original formulation? How do you suppose Freud would object to each adaptation?

2. Suppose you were faced with an extremely difficult final exam, and in order to reduce the anxiety over the exam you use one of the coping strategies described in Table 6.1 on page 158 of the text. Consider each of the descriptive statements and determine which one would fit you in this situation. What strategy would you be using?

3. Consider avoidance strategies as a means of reducing anxiety. Describe two situations in which avoidance would be an effective coping strategy.

4. Discuss the results of the research on displacement using a shock apparatus. What were the central questions of this research? Summarize the findings. Do frustrations always lead to some kind of aggression? Speculate about the ethical dilemmas posed by the method of this research.

5. Specify the improvements of the four-category model of attachment styles over the three-category model. If you believe there are none, state why not. Does the four category model include all the possible styles of adult attachment? Support your answer with examples of people you know or relationships you've been in.

Chapter **7**

The Trait Approach:
Theory, Application, and Assessment

Chapter Outline

The Trait Approach
    Personality as Trait Dimensions
    Special Features of the Trait Approach
Important Trait Theorists
    Gordon Allport
        Nomothetic Versus Idiographic Approaches to Personality
        Functional Autonomy and the Proprium
    Henry Murray
Factor Analysis and the Search for the Structure of Personality
    The Big Five
    Criticism and Limitations of the Big Five Model
The Situation Versus Trait Controversy
    Criticisms of the Trait Approach
        Trait Measures Do Not Predict Behavior Well
        There Is Little Evidence for Cross-Situational Consistency
    In Defense of Personality Traits
        Aggression Data
        Identifying Relevant Traits
        The Importance of 10% of the Variance
    Current Status of the Trait Debate
Application: The Big Five in the Workplace
Assessment: Self-Report Inventories
    The Minnesota Multiphasic Personality Inventory
    Problems with Self-Report Inventories
        Faking
        Carelessness and Sabotage
        Response Tendencies
Strengths and Criticisms of the Trait Approach

Learning Objectives

1. Discuss the reasons why personality researchers today do not use a strict type approach to personality.
2. State the characteristics of the trait approach to personality and distinguish the special features of the trait approach from other approaches to personality. Include the major advantages of studying personality through the trait approach.
3. Discuss the contributions of Gordon Allport to understanding personality and explain why his work was "ground-breaking." Distinguish between nomothetic and idiographic approaches. Identify the three kinds of personality traits proposed by Allport.
4. Define and discuss the terms functional autonomy and proprium. Explain how Allport's approach differs from the psychoanalytic approach with respect to childhood experiences.
5. Discuss the contributions of Henry Murray to understanding personality. Give the name of Murray's approach and discuss the kinds of needs he considered central to personality. Define the concept press and give examples of two kinds of press.
6. Explain how the traits that make up personality are organized into a structure. List and define the factors identified by researchers as the Big Five. Discuss some criticisms and limitations of the Big Five Model of personality structure.
7. Summarize the situation versus trait controversy. Discuss two criticisms of the trait approach given by Mischel with respect to this controversy. Give a defense of the trait approach and explain how the criticisms and defense have improved our understanding of personality traits.
8. Discuss how the Big Five Model is applied in work settings. State the relative desirability of different personality characteristics for the workplace.
9. Explain why self-report inventories are so popular. Describe the Minnesota Multiphasic Personality Inventory and state what psychologists look at in the resulting scores. List three problems associated with self-report inventories and give an example for each.
10. Give three strengths of the trait approach to personality. State why the trait approach is an important theoretical perspective. State the general criticisms that have been made of the trait approach.

Important Concepts

trait (p. 181)
central traits (p. 185)
secondary traits (p. 185)
cardinal traits (p. 186)

nomothetic approach (p. 185)
idiographic approach (p. 185)
functional autonomy (p. 186)
proprium (p. 187)

personology (p. 187)
viscerogenic need (p. 187)
psychogenic need (p. 187)
factor analysis (p. 192)
source traits (p. 192)
Big Five (p. 194)
situationism (p. 199)
person-by-situation approach (p. 199)
aggregate data (p. 201)
variance accounted (p. 203)

press (p. 190)
alpha press (p. 190)
beta press (p. 190)
neuroticism (p. 195)
extraversion (p. 195)
openness (p. 195)
agreeableness (p. 195)
conscientiousness (p. 195)
MMPI (p. 207)
social desirability (p. 211)

Programmed Review

The first attempt to identify and describe relatively stable features of personality was to develop _____ systems.

typology   p. 180

Trait psychologists are more likely to be _____ than practicing therapists.

academic researchers   p. 182

The nomothetic approach to personality measurement looks at _____ traits.

common   p. 185

Allport argued that there is no reason to assume the adult behavior stems from the same motives as earlier behavior because in adulthood behavior has become _____ .

functionally autonomous   p. 186

The _____ is a term used to describe all aspects of the self united under a single concept.

proprium   p. 187

According to Murray, each of us can be described in terms of a personal _____ .

hierarchy of needs   p. 187

Cattell argued that psychologists should not begin with a _____ list of personality traits.

preconceived   p. 190

To discover the structure of personality Cattell used a statistical technique called _____ .

factor analysis   p. 192

The _____ dimension of the Big Five categorizes people according to their level of emotional stability and personal adjustment.

neuroticism   p. 195

People high on the _____ dimension are helpful and sympathetic.

agreeableness   p. 195

When _____ terms are included in the factor analysis of personality, two additional personality factors emerge.

evaluative   p. 196

Advocates of _____ argue that the situation determines behavior almost exclusively.

situationism   p. 199

Today most psychologists agree that the person and the situation _____ to determine behavior.

interact   p. 199

A behavior score based on one measure is low in the concept of psychological testing called _____ .

reliability   p. 201

Employers have used scores from _____ to make hiring and promotion decisions for many years.

personality tests   p. 204

_____ are more widely used today than any other form of personality assessment.

Self-report inventories   p. 206

The extent to which people present themselves in a favorable light is called _____ .

social desirability   p. 211

Social desirability scores are useful when testing the _____ validity of new personality measures.

discriminant   p. 212

Multiple Choice Questions

1. A trait is a dimension of personality used to
   a. measure the instability of personality over time.
   b. categorize people according to the type of personality they possess.
   c. categorize people according to the extent to which they have a characteristic.
   d. predict behavior in specific circumstances.

2. Which of the following is true about the trait approach?
   a. No major schools of psychotherapy have evolved from the trait approach.
   b. The trait approach is the best approach for predicting change in personality.
   c. Many trait researchers do not focus on predicting behavior.
   d. Trait theorists place the most emphasis on identifying the mechanisms that determine behavior.

3. The major trait theorists went beyond the examination of a few traits and
   a. described the nature of the unconscious.
   b. explained the relationship between the person and the situation.
   c. described the structure of personality.
   d. explained the biological contributions to personality.

4. An advantage of using an idiographic approach to personality is that
   a. researchers can compare all people on measures of a certain trait.
   b. the person rather than the researcher determines what traits to examine.
   c. it provides information about the relationship between traits and behavior.
   d. it reveals common traits.

5. According to Allport, a single trait that dominates our personality is called a
   a. central trait.
   b. focal trait.
   c. proprium.
   d. cardinal trait.

6. Which neo-Freudian theorist had the greatest influence on Murray's approach?
   a. Fromm
   b. Erikson
   c. Horney
   d. Jung

7. Which of the following is an example of a psychogenic need?
   a. food
   b. warmth
   c. affiliation
   d. sexual intercourse

8. The environmental forces that interact with needs to determine behavior is the concept introduced by Murray as
   a. cardinal traits.
   b. press.
   c. viscerogenic needs.
   d. idiographic needs.

9. According to Cattell, _____ traits are traits that ultimately constitute the human personality.
   a. cardinal
   b. source
   c. secondary
   d. factor

10. Which of the following is *not* a factor among the Big Five?
    a. psychoticism
    b. neuroticism
    c. openness
    d. agreeableness

11. Steven is a college sophomore who likes to go to the weekly campus lecture series and take courses outside of his major. Given this information, trait researchers would classify Steven as high in
    a. neuroticism.
    b. agreeableness,
    c. openness.
    d. achievement.

12. One of the Big Five dimensions of personality that ranges from organized and determined to careless and easily distracted is the _____ dimension.
    a. agreeableness
    b. extraversion
    c. stick-to-it
    d. conscientiousness

13. The use of trait measures has been embraced by psychologists working in which of the following settings?
    a. education
    b. diagnosis
    c. research
    d. all of the above

14. According to Mischel, the trait approach
    a. is the basis for decisions of little consequence to the person.
    b. does not predict behavior well.
    c. provides evidence of consistency of behaviors across situations.
    d. all of the above

15. Epstein has argued that the reason many researchers fail to produce strong links between personality traits and behavior is that
    a. they don't measure behavior correctly.
    b. they don't measure personality traits correctly.
    c. they don't perform the correct statistical analysis.
    d. none of the above

16. Rosenthal, who compared the amount of variance accounted for in personality research to variance accounted in other fields, found little evidence for a correlation between
    a. smoking and heart attack.
    b. taking aspirin and heart attack.
    c. alcohol abuse and heart attack.
    d. taking AZT and heart attack.

17. Research has shown that among the Big Five personality factors, the best predictor of performance is
    a. neuroticism.
    b. agreeableness.
    c. conscientiousness.
    d. extraversion.

18. Among the criticisms of the MMPI are questions about
    a. the validity of the scales.
    b. the appropriateness of some of the norm data.
    c. the nature of some of the constructs being measured.
    d. all of the above

19. Which of the following is *not* a problem with self-report inventories?
    a. scoring
    b. carelessness
    c faking
    d. response tendencies

20. In which way is the trait approach similar to other approaches to personality?
    a. Trait theorists tend to be academic researchers.
    b. Trait researchers rarely try to understand the behavior of just one person.
    c. Trait theory has generated a great deal of research.
    d. Trait theorists use objective measures to examine their constructs.

Answers to Multiple Choice Questions

1. c, 181
2. a, 182
3. c, 183
4. b, 185
5. d, 186
6. d, 187
7. c, 187
8. b, 190
9. b, 192
10. a, 194
11. c, 195
12. d, 195
13. d, 198
14. b, 198
15. a, 201
16. b, 203
17. c, 205
18. d, 209
19. a, 209
20. c, 215

Integrative Questions

1. Discuss several ways in which the trait approach differs from other approaches to personality. Who is studied? What do trait theorists try to describe and predict? What do trait theorists have to say about personality change?

2. List three fundamental ways in which Allport disagreed with Freud. What alternative explanations for adult behavior and personality did Allport propose?

3. Following the description in the textbook, describe the general process of factor analysis. What is the result of such an analysis? What did Cattell discover concerning the structure of personality using this technique?

4. List and describe each of the personality dimensions known as the Big Five. How would you describe the popular comic strip character Charlie Brown in terms of the Big Five and why?

5. How do modern personality psychologists answer the question of whether personality or situations determine behavior? Give the reasons why we can say there is little evidence for cross-situational consistency. Explain in your own words why personality researchers have failed to find a strong link between personality and behavior.

6. Why are self-report inventories so popular as a means of assessing personality traits? Describe the differences between self-reports and other personality tests such as projective tests and behavioral observation.

7. List and discuss the advantages of the trait approach to personality. What are the basic criticisms of this approach? Is it a problem that there is no single framework or theory of personality traits on which psychologists agree? Is the fact that the trait approach has not generated a school of psychotherapy a problem? Why or why not?

Evaluative Questions

1. Gordon Allport said, "Psychologists would do well to give full recognition to manifest motives before probing the unconscious." State in a paragraph what you think Allport meant by this statement. Of Freud and Allport, who acknowledged the limitations of his theory? What were some of the limitations acknowledged?

2. Describe yourself in terms of the hierarchy of needs proposed by Murray. Give an example from your own experience over the past two months of an alpha press and a beta press and how each worked with your needs to determine your behavior.

3. Given the evidence in favor of the Big Five Model of personality, why would trait theorists not be better off examining only those five main traits? Give two criticisms of the Big Five Model and a response to these criticisms. What is your position on the Big Five Model?

4. Where does your opinion fall in the person versus situation controversy? Do you think it is appropriate to make decisions about mental health or employment decisions based solely on personality test scores? Why or why not?

Chapter **8**

The Trait Approach: Relevant Research

Chapter Outline

The Need for Achievement
    High Need for Achievement Characteristics
    Predicting Achievement Behavior
    Gender, Culture, and Achievement
    Cognitive Variables and the Attributional Approach to Achievement Motivation
Type A--Type B Behavior Patterns
    Type A as a Personality Variable
    Type A and Achievement
    Type A Behavior and Health Revisited
        Measuring Type A: A Question of Validity
        Identifying the "Toxic Component"
Social Anxiety
    Characteristics of Socially Anxious People
    Explaining Social Anxiety
Emotions
    Emotional Affectivity
    Emotional Intensity
    Emotional Expressiveness
Optimism and Pessimism
    Dealing with Adversity
    Defensive Pessimism

Learning Objectives

1. Describe what is meant by the trait called need for Achievement with an example. List the characteristics of people with high need for Achievement.

2. State how need for Achievement can be predicted from what parents do. Explain how need for Achievement is related to both gender and culture.

3. Discuss the attributional approach to achievement motivation and describe the three dimensions that determine the kind of attributions a person makes.

4. Define Type A and Type B behavior. List the many ways in which Type A people differ from Type B people. Discuss the relationship between Type A behavior and achievement and the potential liabilities of being Type A.

5. Specify how Type A behavior can impact one's health. Discuss the problems of validity associated with measuring Type A and a solution to the problem of identifying the toxic component of Type A.

6. Define social anxiety and distinguish it from other kinds of anxiety. List and discuss the characteristics of socially anxious people.

7. State the ways in which personality psychologists have explained social anxiety. Discuss the evidence for evaluation apprehension and for other causes of social anxiety.

8. Define and distinguish among three aspects of emotion that are also personality traits. Describe the characteristics of each dimension of emotion.

9. Define optimism and pessimism. Discuss how optimistic and pessimistic people use different coping strategies to deal with anxiety. Define dispositional optimism and state the advantages of being optimistic. Define defensive pessimism and state its advantages.

Important Concepts

need for Achievement (p. 220)
entrepreneurial behavior (p. 221)
control (p. 228)
coronary-prone behavior pattern (p. 229)
competitive achievement striving (p. 230)
"toxic component" (p. 235)
social anxiety (p. 237)
evaluation apprehension (p. 241)
affect intensity (p. 246)
dispositional optimism (p. 251)
defensive pessimism (p. 254)

attributions (p. 227)
stability (p. 228)
locus (p. 228)
Type A--Type B (p. 229)
time urgency (p. 230)
hostility (p. 235)
emotional affectivity (p. 243)
positive affect (p. 243)
negative affect (p. 243)
emotional expressiveness (p. 248)

Programmed Review

For many psychologists personality research has become synonymous with the _____ and examination of traits.

measurement   p. 218

Concepts like need for Achievement fit well with the American concern for _____ and success in business.

economic growth   p. 221

The opportunity to receive concrete _____ about their performance is important to high-need achievers.

feedback   p. 221

Research suggests that too much parental involvement can stifle children's sense of _____ .

independence   p. 222

Presidents whose inaugural speeches indicated a high need for Achievement usually are rated by historians as _____ .

ineffective leaders   p. 223

With respect to gender, nearly all of McClelland's research was conducted on _____ .

males   p. 226

The meaning of _____ can vary as a function of culture.

achievement   p. 227

According to the attribution approach to achievement motivation, we often ask ourselves _____ we have done as well as we have.

why   p. 227

An easy way to improve achievement motivation is to change people's _____ .

attributions   p. 228

Type A people often find _____ people a source of frustration.

easygoing   p. 230

Type A people often deal with arousal due to physiological stress by _____ .

denial   p. 231

The most popular self-report measure of Type A--Type B personality is _____ .

the Jenkins Activity Survey   p. 234

People high in _____ might become very upset when they are stuck in a slow-moving line.

hostility   p. 235

Most researchers today appear to use the terms social anxiety and _____ synonymously.

shyness   p. 238

Socially anxious people tend to interpret feedback they get in a _____ .

negative light.   p. 240

Shy persons' social interaction style is a type of _____ .

self-protective strategy   p. 242

Researchers have used the _____ technique to examine the relation among various emotions.

factor analysis   p. 243

Affect intensity refers to the _____ to which people typically experience their emotions.

degree (strength)   p. 246

Heart transplant patients with positive expectations do better _____ to life after surgery than those with a pessimistic outlook.

adjusting   p. 250

Defensive pessimists generate their gloomy expectations as part of a deliberate _____ for dealing with upcoming events.

strategy   p. 254

Multiple Choice Questions

1. Research on Type A behavior began as
   a. a study of individual differences in personality and later became useful in applied areas.
   b. an important means of understanding social anxiety.
   c. an applied concept and later came under the study of academic researchers.
   d. an example of a defense mechanism.

2. Like other trait measures, need for Achievement scores are
   a. assumed to reflect a biological contribution to personality.
   b. not at all predictive of behavior patterns.
   c. assumed to reflect relatively stable individual differences.
   d. not at all reliable for the purposes of diagnosis.

3. Which of the following is indicative of high need for Achievement?
   a. a student who is motivated to avoid failure on an exam
   b. a business person who takes chances to get ahead
   c. a gambler who will only bet on a sure thing
   d. an employee who works hard at very boring tasks

4. Good advice for parents who want to raise their children to have a high need for Achievement is to
   a. continue giving encouragement and support in every activity of the child.
   b. involve themselves in all of the child's interests.
   c. not give the child rewards for personal accomplishments.
   d. find a balance between encouragement and robbing the child of initiative.

5. Which of the following measures did McClelland use to study the level of achievement emphasized by different cultures?
   a. themes in children's books
   b. economic development
   c. amount of electricity used
   d. all of the above

6. As career aspirations for women have changed over the past few decades,
    a. women have been more successful in the business world.
    b. we have see a decrease in need for Achievement among females.
    c. opportunities for women have not changed.
    d. all of the above

7. Which of the following is true about gender and achievement?
    a. Women and men act similarly in achievement settings.
    b. Men and women differ in the way they define success.
    c. Women in our society are more likely to see success in terms of external standards.
    d. Men and women assign similar values to achievement tasks.

8. Which of the following is *not* a dimension of attributions?
    a. reliability
    b. stability
    c. locus
    d. control

9. An early term for Type A behavior patterns was the _____ behavior pattern.
    a. time-wasting
    b. energy-consuming
    c. coronary-prone
    d. cancer-causing

10. Jerry and George work for an advertising agency in Chicago. Jerry has been classified as Type A and George has been labeled Type B by their employer. Which of the following is a likely difference between Jerry and George?
    a. George works harder than Jerry but does not receive as much reward for his work.
    b. Jerry deals with frustrating situations with aggressiveness.
    c. George believes that time is important and shouldn't be wasted.
    d. Jerry does not procrastinate as often as George.

11. When participants in a study of arousal were asked to repeat lists of two, five, or seven numbers in backward order,
    a. the most difficult task aroused Type B participants more than Type A.
    b. the most difficult task aroused Type A participants more than Type B.
    c. regardless of the difficulty, Type B participants were more aroused than Type A.
    d. arousal levels did not differ between easy and difficult tasks.

12. According to laboratory experiments that examine how Type A and Type B people respond to achievement tasks, the single best way to motivate a Type A person is
    a. by giving them plenty of time to perform a task.
    b. the opportunity to be challenged.
    c. by setting up a situation of competition.
    d. by making the task an easy one.

13. Most of the failure to uncover a significant relationship between Type A behavior and heart disease occurred when investigators used
    a. behavioral observation.
    b. self-report inventories.
    c. the Thematic Apperception Test.
    d. none of the above

14. Researchers investigating social anxiety have consistently found that about _____ of the people surveyed identify themselves as shy.
    a. 40%
    b. 30%
    c. 20%
    d. 15%

15. Which of the following statements is true about social anxiety?
    a. Socially anxious people recognize the source of their anxiety.
    b. Social anxiety can result from anticipated social interactions.
    c. We can identify a relatively stable tendency for people to experience social anxiety.
    d. all of the above

16. Shy people are more likely than nonshy people to
    a. become psychotic.
    b. become aggressive.
    c. blush.
    d. forget.

17. In a study in which participants were asked to engage in a five-minute "get acquainted" conversation, researchers found that
    a. socially anxious people were less likely to agree with the other person.
    b. little attempt was made by shy people to be polite to the other person.
    c. shy people attempt to minimize the amount of evaluation by the other person.
    d. all of the above

18. Lisa frequently experiences nervousness in her job and can become angry when the pressures of her work increase. Which dimension of emotion is illustrated by Lisa's behavior at work?
    a. positive affect
    b. negative affect
    c. intensity
    d. expressiveness

19. Which of the following has been demonstrated by research on emotional affectivity?
    a. Negative affect is related to psychological stress.
    b. People with positive affect report more health problems.
    c. Negative affect is related to social activity.
    d. all of the above

20. Emotional expressiveness refers to a person's _____ of emotions.
    a. strength
    b. memory
    c. inner conflict
    d. outward display

21. Which of the following is true about emotional expressiveness?
    a. The more expressive of emotions the fewer problems in romantic relationships.
    b. Highly expressive people tend to have higher self-esteem.
    c. Women tend to be more expressive than men.
    d. all of the above

22. Which of the following is a reason why defensive pessimists deliberately take a pessimistic approach?
    a. to set themselves up for success
    b. to prepare themselves for failure
    c. to reduce the need to try harder
    d. to make themselves fear success

23. When defensive pessimists are allowed to worry about an upcoming test, they _____ than people not allowed to worry.
    a. performed worse
    b. felt better
    c. experienced more anxiety
    d. became more optimistic

Answers to Multiple Choice Questions

1.	c, 219	10.	d, 230	19.	a, 244
2.	c, 220	11.	b, 231	20.	d, 249
3.	a, 221	12.	c, 233	21.	d, 249
4.	d, 222	13.	b, 234	22.	b, 254
5.	d, 224	14.	a, 237	23.	b, 255
6.	a, 226	15.	d, 237		
7.	b, 226	16.	c, 240		
8.	a, 228	17.	c, 241		
9.	c, 229	18.	b, 243		

Integrative Questions

1. Give your own description of a person with a high need for Achievement. How is need for Achievement like other trait measures? What kinds of careers and jobs are best suited for those with high achievement motivation? Does high need for Achievement always lead to success in the workplace?

2. With respect to gender and achievement motivation, what questions are asked and not asked by researchers? What standards of success should researchers apply to achievement settings? Explain how different cultures define success.

3. What kind of people are likely to have a heart attack? What are the three major components of the personality of such people? State the one underlying concept proposed by Glass on which all three dimensions of attribution may rest. Give one piece of evidence to support the idea of one single concept.

4. Give two reasons why measures of Type A behavior do not always predict health problems. Explain what is meant by "toxic component" and state whether or not researchers have found it. If so, what is it?

5. What are the differences between introversion and shyness? List all of the characteristics you have learned about social anxiety.

6. Contrast the research presented in the text between evaluation apprehension as a cause of social anxiety and other possible causes. What do therapy programs do to help people overcome their shyness?

7. In what ways are people with high emotional intensity similar to those with low emotional intensity? What is the relationship between emotional expressiveness and successful romantic relationships?

8. State the advantages and disadvantages of dispositional optimism. What are some of the differences between optimists and pessimists when faced with stressful events? What coping strategies do these two kinds of personalities use?

Evaluative Questions

1. Suppose you are looking for a full-time job. Based on your personal assessment of your level of need for Achievement, what kinds of jobs would be a good fit to your personality? List three different occupations in which you can succeed.

2. According to research by McClelland, the number of achievement themes in children's stories in a culture was correlated with levels of electricity usage. Given this result, why should we be careful not to conclude that achievement themes cause differences in electricity use? That is, consider other explanations for McClelland's results.

3. Suppose you work in human resources for a large company as an interviewer of applicants for jobs. Your task is to determine those applicants who have a high need for Achievement. For each of the following interview questions, give a model response of an applicant with high achievement motivation.
    a. What are your career goals?
    b. What have you failed at and how have you handled that failure?
    c. How did you decide to go into this field?

4. Think about the most recent exam you had to take in college. Based on your experience on that exam, what attributions do you make for your success or failure? Where do your attributions fall along the three dimensions of stability, locus, and control? What does this mean to you and your future behavior?

5. Consider someone you know who many would agree is a shy person. Identify the situations in which you think the person is most shy. Could evaluation apprehension be the reason for social anxiety? Specify the ways in which the person fits the characteristics of socially anxious people.

6. At this very moment, how would you classify yourself according to the information presented in Figure 8.2 of the text? To what degree do these dimensions have predictive validity?

7. Define the three aspects of emotion known as affectivity, intensity, and expressiveness. State how these qualities of emotion can be personality traits. Give an example of each dimension that illustrates the characteristics of each and distinguishes among them.

8. In your own opinion, what is the ethical status of the research in which participants were deliberately exposed to cold and flu viruses?

Chapter **9**

The Biological Approach: Theory, Application, and Assessment

Chapter Outline

Hans Eysenck's Theory of Personality
    The Structure of Personality
    A Biological Basis for Personality
Temperament
    The EAS Temperament Model
    Inhibited and Uninhibited Children
Evolutionary Personality Psychology
    Natural Selection and Psychological Mechanisms
    Anxiety and Social Exclusion
Application: Children's Temperaments and School
    Temperament and Academic Performance
    The "Goodness of Fit" Model
Assessment: Brain Electrical Activity and Cerebral Asymmetry
    Measuring Brain Activity
    Cerebral Asymmetry
    Individual Differences in Cerebral Asymmetry
Strengths and Criticisms of the Biological Approach

Learning Objectives

1. Describe the history of the study of biological influence on personality. State why the "blank slate" view is no longer supported by psychologists.

2. Discuss Eysenck's theory of personality and summarize his view of biology's role in human personality by discussing the structure of personality.

3. State the ways in which extraverts and introverts differ. State how they are similar. Give three arguments made by Eysenck for the biological basis of personality.

4. Define temperaments. Discuss how temperaments develop into personality traits. State the behavior that temperament researchers find most important.

5. List and define the three general dispositions proposed in the EAS temperament model. Give a reason why general dispositions at childhood set the direction for adult personality traits.

6. Distinguish between inhibited and uninhibited children. Discuss the stability of these tendencies as the child develops into an adult.

7. State the basic tenets of evolutionary personality psychology. Describe the role of natural selection and the psychological mechanisms that determine personality.

8. Explain how human characteristics like anxiety could have evolved. State the role of social exclusion in the evolution of human anxiety.

9. Describe how inhibited and uninhibited children respond to their first day of school. Define and contrast the three basic patterns of behavior in school children.

10. Discuss the impact of temperament on how well a child does in school. Give reasons for the relationship between temperament and school performance. Explain what is meant by the "Goodness of Fit" model and provide a strategy for improving teaching based on it.

11. Discuss the nature of EEG research on personality and emotion and describe cerebral asymmetry. Explain how emotion is predicted by individual differences in cerebral asymmetry and the possible role of thresholds in brain activity.

12. Give three strengths of the biological approach to personality. State how this approach serves as a bridge between personality psychology and biology.

13. Summarize the criticisms that can be made of the biological approach to personality. State whether each criticism is a methodological limitation or a general theoretical consideration.

Important Concepts

specific response level (p. 261)
habitual response (p. 261)
extraversion (p. 261)
neuroticism (p. 265)
psychoticism (p. 265)
anxiety to novelty (p. 272)
evolutionary personality theory (p. 275)
natural selection (p. 275)
easy child (p. 279)
difficult child (p. 279)
slow-to-warm-up child (p. 279)

supertrait (p. 261)
temperaments (p. 267)
emotionality (p. 270)
activity (p. 270)
sociability (p. 270)
inhibited/uninhibited children (p. 271)
social exclusion (p. 277)
Goodness of Fit Model (p. 281)
electroencephalograph (p. 283)
alpha wave (p. 284)
cerebral asymmetry (p. 284)

Programmed Review

There is a growing recognition that personality cannot be separated from _____ factors.

biological								p. 260

Eysenck argues that extraverts and introverts differ both in their behavior and in their _____ makeup.

physiological								p. 264

_____ refers to the intensity of one's emotional reactions.

Emotionality								p. 270

Temperament researchers argue that both level of emotionality and _____ influence the course of personality development.

environment								p. 270

A specific form of anxiety generated by unfamiliar people, settings, or challenges is called _____ .

anxiety to novelty							p. 272

Parents of _____ children can do their child a favor by becoming sensitive to the child's discomfort in unfamiliar settings.

inhibited								p. 274

Proponents of evolutionary personality theory use the process of _____ to explain universal human characteristics.

natural selection							p. 275

Opportunities for learning and achievement in school may be shaped by the child's _____ .

temperament								p. 280

The _____ child is typically low in adaptability and in a negative mood.

difficult								p. 279

Students get higher grades and better evaluations from teachers when the student's temperament matches the teacher's _____ .

expectations (demands)   p. 281

Researchers measure brain activity with an instrument called an _____ .

electroencephalograph (EEG)   p. 283

The difference in right and left hemisphere activity is referred to as _____ by researchers.

cerebral asymmetry   p. 284

Some researchers explain findings of cerebral asymmetry in terms of _____ .

thresholds   p. 285

One of the most important messages from the biological approach is that we need to be more aware of the _____ on how much we can change personality.

limitations   p. 288

Multiple Choice Questions

1. The growing acceptance of the biological influences on personality is partly
   a. due to a return to the notion of the blank slate.
   b. a reflection of the decline of psychoanalysis in academic psychology.
   c. a reflection of behaviorism's decline in academic psychology.
   d. due to computer technology of the late 20th century.

2. The most basic structure in Eysenck's model of personality structure is the
   a. habitual response level.
   b. specific response level.
   c. supertrait level.
   d. temperament level.

3. Sherry has many friends and enjoys purchasing gifts for them on impulse. She gets excited when she surprises her friends with these gifts. Her behavior suggests that she is at the high end on the _____ supertrait dimension.
   a. extraversion
   b. neuroticism
   c. psychoticism
   d. sentimentalism

4. Which of the following is *not* a basic disposition proposed by Buss and Plomin?
   a. activity
   b. connectivity
   c. emotionality
   d. sociability

5. According to Kagan, children who are inhibited react to unfamiliar situations with
   a. excitement.
   b. fear.
   c. curiosity.
   d. caution.

6. Which of the following is a physical difference between inhibited and uninhibited children?
   a. susceptibility to allergies
   b. body build
   c. eye color
   d. all of the above

7. According to evolutionary personality psychologists, social rejection leads to social anxiety because
   a. people fear that others will punish them.
   b. each of us are reminded of a traumatic experience in childhood.
   c. experiencing anxiety serves an important survival function.
   d. all of the above

8. Among the psychological mechanisms identified by evolutionary psychologists as resulting from the natural selection process is
   a. anger.
   b. ambivalence.
   c. arrogance.
   d. all of the above

9. Arguments given for the evolution of anxiety include all but which of the following?
   a. a need to belong to groups
   b. a need to dominate others
   c. anxiety is found in nearly all cultures
   d. anxiety meets the survival needs of the species

10. Which of the following is *not* a temperamental difference found to affect how a child performs in school?
    a. approach or withdrawal
    b. distractibility
    c. attention to details
    d. adaptability

11. Larry is in kindergarten and shows signs of being inhibited. He is reluctant to engage in new activities and slow to adapt to new tasks given by his teacher. Larry is probably
    a. an easy child.
    b. a slow-to-warm-up child.
    c. a difficult child.
    d. a fast-to-cool-down child.

12. Which of the following is false about differences in temperament patterns in children?
    a. Differences show up on teachers' evaluations.
    b. Differences are found in the child's grades.
    c. Differences are found in scores on achievement tests.
    d. Differences are related to intelligence.

13. Differences in temperament can influence a student's grades depending on
    a. the student's level of brain activity.
    b. the student's level of ability.
    c. the teacher's expectations.
    d. the teacher's self-esteem.

14. Which of the following is an advantage of using the electroencephalograph (EEG)?
    a. It allows researchers to record brain activity in long intervals.
    b. The electrode paste that is used is not messy.
    c. The procedure is not uncomfortable.
    d. It is a complex procedure that allows the participant's hair to grow back.

15. Using the electroencephalograph (EEG), researchers have found higher activation in the left hemisphere is associated with
    a. negative mood.
    b. feelings of happiness.
    c. greater reactions to films that elicit fear.
    d. feelings of disgust.

16. A strength of the biological approach is that
    a. it has succeeded in identifying specific parameters for psychologists who want to change behavior.
    b. there seems to be no limit to psychologists' ability to test for biological factors.
    c. most of its advocates are medical doctors with an interest in treating disease.
    d. it makes a variety of suggestions for personality change.

Answers to Multiple Choice Questions

1.	c, 260	9.	b, 277
2.	b, 261	10.	c, 279
3.	a, 261	11.	b, 279
4.	b, 269	12.	d, 280
5.	d, 271	13.	c, 281
6.	d, 273	14.	c, 283
7.	c, 275	15.	b, 284
8.	a, 276	16.	a, 286

Integrative Questions

1. How does a complete understanding of human personality require us to go beyond the traditional boundaries of personality psychology? Specify how Eysenck's theory goes beyond those traditional boundaries. What aspects of his theory depart from the Freudian approach and the trait approach? In what ways is Eysenck's theory related to these?

2. Discuss how the three general dispositions described by Buss and Plomin translate into adult personality traits. Include in your answer the role of the environment and give a reason why these general dispositions set the direction of adult personality.

3. From the discussion of childhood temperaments given in the text, summarize what parents can do to help their inhibited children and what teachers can do to improve the education of inhibited children.

4. List the psychological mechanisms given in the text that have been identified as resulting from the natural selection process. For each mechanism give the logic behind the idea that it is adaptive for survival.

5. Give an example of how a classroom can be arranged to be more helpful for students with different temperaments. Give examples of how teachers can misinterpret temperamental differences in students.

6. Write a story titled, "The day I was a subject in a study of personality," that describes what would take place if you participated in a study in which your brain activity was measured.

Evaluative Questions

1. What temperaments do you possess? Give personal evidence for your own emotionality, activity, and sociability. Do you think these temperaments were inherited? Why or why not?

2. Describe one study that provides evidence that the temperaments a person has in childhood show up later in life. Consider at least one factor other than a temperaments that may explain the results of the study. State how it could.

3. Specify where evolutionary theory and Freudian theory cross paths.

4. State a definition of the behavior pattern psychologists call altruism. Given that the ultimate expression of altruistic behavior results the sacrifice of one's life, how might an evolutionary personality psychologist explain altruism as a result of natural selection? (Hint: Humans share many genes with siblings and other family members.)

5. Consider the mix of students in your personality class with you. Do you think the temperamental patterns of childhood are still represented to some extent in the young adults in your class? Discuss how far some grade school teachers might go to change their teaching style to be sensitive to those children who are slow to warm up to new tasks. Do the professors at your school show an awareness that not all college students approach school and learning in the same way?

6. Given that anxiety generally prevents humans from behaviors that would lead to social isolation, can we be absolutely sure that anxiety is a biologically-based factor in human personality? Consider the kinds of arguments made by evolutionary personality psychologists for the existence of anxiety.

Chapter **10**

The Biological Approach: Relevant Research

Chapter Outline

Heritability of Personality Traits
    Separating Environmental from Genetic Influences
    Problems with Genetics Research
Extraversion--Introversion
    The Heritability of Extraversion
    Extraversion and Preferred Arousal Level
    Extraversion and Happiness
Evolutionary Personality Theory and Mate Selection
    What Men Look for in Women
    What Women Look for in Men
    Conclusions and Limitations

Learning Objectives

1. State the reasons for the resistance psychologists have shown in accepting the role of biology in personality.

2. Discuss the heritability of personality traits and five different methods used by researchers to separate environmental influences from genetic influences.

3. Specifically discuss the rationale behind the twin-study method and adoption studies of genetic influence.

4. List and describe the problems associated with these methods of genetics research.

5. Discuss the heritability of extraversion and the two main causes of individual differences in extraversion-introversion. Describe the different sources of evidence that suggest these differences are based in biology.

6. Describe the relationship between extraversion and preferred level of arousal. Give the research evidence in support of this relationship.

7. State who is happier among extraverts and introverts and state several reasons for this difference.

8. Discuss the kinds of information researchers have found about gender roles and the nature of romantic relationships.

9. Contrast the basis of mate selection for males with that for females by explaining the different motives men and women have in choosing a mate.

10. Discuss what men look for in women and describe the research that supports the evolutionary basis of mate selection in men.

11. Discuss what women look for in men and describe the research that supports the evolutionary basis of mate selection in women.

12. State the conclusions that can be drawn about gender differences in mate selection and the limitations faced by evolutionary personality researchers who study these differences.

Important Concepts

twin-study method (p. 294)
adoption study (p. 296)
subjective well-being (p. 305)
intrasexual selection (p. 308)

monozygotic twins (p. 294)
dizygotic twins (p. 295)
parental investment (p. 306)

Programmed Review

For technological and ethical reasons, it is not possible to _____ people's genes and observe the kind of adult they become.

manipulate   p. 293

The most popular method used to examine the role of genetics and the environment in personality is the _____ method.

twin-study   p. 294

Adoptions are not _____ events.

random   p. 298

Genetics may influence only certain personality traits and then only during certain _____ of life.

stages   p. 298

Each person born with a predisposition toward introversion will develop a different style of dealing with heightened _____ to stimulation.

sensitivity   p. 299

Research has found that students who prefer a quiet, isolated room were more likely to be _____ .

introverts   p. 302

When given the opportunity, research participants who are introverts tend to set earphones at _____ levels than extraverts.

lower   p. 303

On average extraverts report higher levels of subjective _____ than introverts.

well-being   p. 303

The result of impulsivity is that extraverts experience more _____ than introverts.

mood swings   p. 305

From the evolutionary perspective, choosing a romantic partner is based in part on concerns for _____ .

parental investment   p. 306

The evidence is abundant that men are more likely than women to look at _____ when selecting a dating or marriage partner.

physical attractiveness   p. 307

According to the parental investment analysis, women prefer to mate with men who can _____ for their offspring.

provide   p. 311

Evolutionary personality psychology is limited to _____ mating choices.

heterosexual   p. 314

87

Multiple Choice Questions

1. The question of the origin of personality between genetics and the environment is not *which* of these shapes our personality but rather
   a. to what extent our personalities are shaped by each.
   b. why we have personalities.
   c. what traits can be changed by changing the environment.
   d. who has the better theory of personality development.

2. Siblings' personalities may be similar because
   a. children inherited personality traits from their parents.
   b. siblings share the same living environments during childhood.
   c. siblings are raised in the same way by parents.
   d. all of the above

3. Twins that we commonly call identical twins
   a. are monozygotic.
   b. are dizygotic.
   c. come from different fertilized eggs.
   d. are sometimes called fraternal twins.

4. Behavior genetics researchers have taken their data from twin studies and used formulas to estimate that about _____ of the stability in adult personalities can be attributed to genetics.
   a. 10%
   b. 20%
   c. 30%
   d. 40%

5. Which of the following is a problem for the assumption that MZ and DZ twins are raised in equally similar environments?
   a. DZ twins may be treated more alike than identical twins.
   b. MZ twins purposefully join different clubs and have different friends.
   c. MZ twins may share more of their environment than DZ twins.
   d. all of the above

6. The most problematic assumption in adoption studies is that
   a. biological offspring are more similar to their parents than adopted children.
   b. adopted children have different genes than biological offspring.
   c. parents treat an adopted child in the same way they do their biological offspring.
   d. twins who are adopted by different families share many of the same genes.

7. Research on the genetic heritability of extraversion-introversion has made use of
   a. brain activity measures.
   b. the twin-study method.
   c. differences in sensitivity to stimulation.
   d. only twins that have been reared together (in the same environment).

8. A study of the library rooms preferred by different students demonstrated that
   a. students in a quiet and isolated room were more likely to be extraverts.
   b. when in the library even introverts prefer the opportunity to socialize.
   c. extraverts preferred open rooms more than isolated rooms.
   d. introverts preferred to study in rooms close to an exit.

9. Researchers have found that the one day of the week when extraverts tend to have a better mood than introverts is
   a. Monday
   b. Friday
   c. Saturday
   d. none of the above

10. The fact that friends often serve as an important buffer against stress supports the idea that extraverts
    a. are generally more anxious than introverts.
    b. have higher positive affect due to greater social activity.
    c. are less sensitive to information about rewards than introverts.
    d. often find interacting with friends an unpleasant experience.

11. Why might extraverts not always be happier than introverts?
    a. Extraverts are more likely to be socially active.
    b. Extraverts are more likely to be impulsive.
    c. Introverts do not involve themselves in activities that increase feelings of competence and worth.
    d. Extraverts are more sensitive to positive feedback.

12. Which of the following is true about parental investment?
    a. Males are more selective about whom they choose to mate than females.
    b. Males of many species are free to mate with as many females as they can.
    c. Investment in selecting a mate is larger for males than for females.
    d. Males select mates who are more likely to be good parents.

13. Evolutionary psychologists predict that men look for _____ in women.
    a. age and maturity
    b. financial security
    c. signs of dominance
    d. physical features associated with youth

14. One result of human males' preferences in mate selection is
    a. women compete for a man's attention.
    b. women compete in the workplace.
    c. women brag about their sexual encounters.
    d. all of the above

15. A result of patterns of mate selection by human females is that
    a. men seldom let on what their financial resources may be.
    b. men alter their physical appearance to be more attractive to women.
    c. men compete for a woman's attention.
    d. all of the above

16. With regard to mate selection, one limitation of evolutionary personality theory is that
    a. instincts inherited from our ancestors may overshadow the characteristics men and women look for in some cultures.
    b. researchers cannot manipulate the variables they study.
    c. the methods do not give researchers the ability to make strong predictions.
    d. it assumes a causal relationship between mate selection and environment.

Answers to Multiple Choice Questions

1.	a, 291	9.	d, 303
2.	d, 294	10.	b, 304
3.	a, 294	11.	b, 305
4.	d, 295	12.	b, 306
5.	c, 298	13.	d, 307
6.	c, 298	14.	a, 308
7.	b, 300	15.	c, 311
8.	c, 302	16.	b, 312

Integrative Questions

1. In general, how much of our personalities are inherited from our parents? Describe the logic behind two methods researchers use to determine the relative influence of biology on personality.

2. What assumptions are made about twins that allows researchers to study the biological contributions to personality? Of these assumptions, which are called into question by critics of the biological approach to personality? Discuss four problems associated with genetics research.

3. Discuss the research evidence for the heritability of the extraversion-introversion variable. What features of the Swedish and Finnish samples make them so important for genetics researchers?

4. Discuss the difference in preference for arousal between extraverts and introverts. Which are more sensitive to stimulation, introverts or extraverts? Give two ways in which sensitivity to stimulation translates into behavior. Summarize the research findings on preferred stimulation level.

5. What do men look for in women and what do women look for in men? Give the evolutionary reasons for these differences in mate selection. Offer other evidence in support of evolutionary personality theory in addition to selection based on features of high reproductive value.

6. Give an example of a cultural norm that interferes with the predictions of evolutionary psychology about mate selection.

Evaluative Questions

1. Discuss the logic behind five different methods used by genetics researchers to estimate the heritability of personality. What aspects of these methods are shared and what aspects of each is unique to that method? Give one problem with genetics research and state which of these methods produce estimates that are undermined by the problem.

2. At this moment as you study, do you have the stereo or TV on or off? Or if you are not near a stereo or television, do you prefer some noise or no noise when you are studying? According to research on sensitivity to stimulation, what does your study environment preference tell you about your personality?

3. Who is happier, introverts or extraverts? State the evidence that supports your answer. Discuss one alternative explanation for the differences in reported level of positive mood. Give a rule of thumb for obtaining happiness.

4. Consider the characteristics in men that women look for when selecting a partner. List and discuss those characteristics that do not strictly fit the evolutionary perspective in modern society. Give reasons for departures from the predictions of evolutionary psychology.

5. Critically evaluate the findings of the evolutionary perspective on mate selection. Discuss the kinds of conclusions that can and cannot be drawn about variables such as gender, age, and physical attractiveness.

6. How might the evolutionary perspective explain the mate selection of homosexual men and women?

Chapter 11

The Humanistic Approach: Theory, Application, and Assessment

Chapter Outline

The Roots of Humanistic Psychology
Key Elements of the Humanistic Approach
    Personal Responsibility
    The Here and Now
    The Phenomenology of the Individual
    Personal Growth
Carl Rogers
    The Fully Functioning Person
    Anxiety and Defense
    Conditions of Worth and Unconditional Positive Regard
Abraham Maslow
    Motivation and the Hierarchy of Needs
        Maslow's Need Hierarchy
            Physiological Needs
            Safety Needs
            Belongingness and Love Needs
            Esteem Needs
            Need for Self-Actualization
        Misconceptions and Maslow's Need Hierarchy
    The Study of Psychologically Healthy People
The Psychology of Optimal Experience
    Optimal Experience
    Optimal Experience and Happiness in Everyday Activities
Application: Person-Centered Therapy and Job Satisfaction
    Person-Centered Therapy
    Job Satisfaction and the Hierarchy of Needs
Assessment: The Q-Sort Technique
Strengths and Criticisms of the Humanistic Approach

Learning Objectives

1. Relate the historical roots of humanistic psychology, both in terms of earlier approaches to personality and philosophical influences. Include in the discussion what is meant by "third force" in American psychology.

2. List and briefly explain the four key elements of the humanistic approach to personality. State why each is important to the approach.

3. Discuss the basic tenets of Carl Rogers' humanistic approach. Describe his characterization of the fully functioning person.

4. Explain where anxiety comes from according to Rogers. Discuss the defenses that Rogers suggested we use against anxiety. Define conditions of worth and specify the importance of unconditional positive regard for the person's self-concept.

5. Discuss the central concepts of Abraham Maslow's theory of personality. Contrast his conception of the human with the Freud's view. List and define each of the five levels in Maslow's hierarchy of needs.

6. Define self-actualization and discuss the common misconceptions people have about Maslow's need hierarchy.

7. Describe how Maslow went about studying psychologically healthy people. List each of the characteristics of the individual who is self-actualized.

8. Discuss the concept of optimal experience. List and define the eight characteristics of flow experiences identified by Csikszentmihalyi. Specify in what everyday activities people are more likely to have flow experiences.

9. Describe the person-centered approach to psychotherapy. Indicate the significance of the proper relationship in the therapeutic setting by discussing the elements that Rogers suggested are necessary for a therapeutic relationship to exist.

10. Explain how Maslow's need hierarchy can be used to account for job satisfaction. Discuss the idea of Eupsychian management.

11. Describe the Q-Sort technique of assessment and explain how it is used to track progress during psychotherapy. Discuss the different correlational outcomes of the Q-Sort depending on the agreement of clients' real and ideal selves.

12. Discuss the influences that the humanistic approach to personality has had on psychology and psychotherapy.

13. State five criticisms that have been made against humanistic psychology. Explain why the usefulness of humanistic psychotherapy is limited in its effectiveness.

Important Concepts

"third force" (p. 317)
personal responsibility (p. 319)
the here and now (p. 320)
phenomenology (p. 320)
subception (p. 324)
conditional positive regard (p. 325)
unconditional positive regard (p. 326)
deficiency motive (p. 328)
growth need (p. 328)
belongingness and love needs (p. 330)
esteem needs (p. 331)
self-actualization (p. 332)
enculturalization (p. 334)
peak experiences (p. 334)
person-centered therapy (p. 339)
Eupsychian management (p. 342)

existential psychologists (p. 318)
personal growth (p. 321)
fully functioning person (p. 323)
distortion (p. 324)
denial (p. 324)
disorganization (p. 325)
conditions of worth (p. 325)
hierarchy of needs (p. 329)
physiological needs (p. 329)
safety needs (p. 329)
holistic analysis (p. 333)
self-actualizing creativity (p. 334)
optimal experience (p. 336)
flow (p. 336)
Q-Sort (p. 343)

Programmed Review

Important aspects of human personality such as _____ were missing from the Freudian and behavioristic approaches.

free will and human dignity   p. 317

Whereas psychoanalysts emphasize that adult personalities are formed in childhood, humanistic therapists focus on _____ .

the here and now   p. 320

Carl Rogers pioneered humanistic psychotherapy with his _____ approach.

person-centered   p. 321

The most common defense, according to Rogers, is the process of _____ .

distortion   p. 324

According to Maslow, the motive that results from a lack of some object is called a _____ motive.

deficiency   p. 328

The second level of Maslow's hierarchy is the _____ needs.

safety p. 329

Maslow believed very few people reach _____, which is the point at which their potential is fully developed.

self-actualization p. 332

Because of their self-acceptance, self-actualized people do not feel _____ about the bad things they have done.

guilty p. 333

People report that during optimal experiences they feel as if they are caught in natural and _____ movement from one step to the next.

effortless p. 336

In person-centered therapy, the therapists job is to allow the client to get back on a _____ and to continue progressing.

positive growth track p. 339

Research has confirmed that the amount of satisfaction we get from our job is related to the amount of satisfaction we have in _____ .

our life generally p. 342

Maslow's work has influenced the way many _____ psychologists look at job satisfaction.

organizational p. 342

A tool of assessment used by Rogers and other humanistic therapists is the _____ .

Q-Sort p. 343

In the late 1970s many converts to the humanistic approach became _____ as some humanistically oriented programs were declared failures.

disenchanted p. 347

One criticism of the humanistic approach to personality is that many key concepts are _____ .

poorly defined   p. 348

Multiple Choice Questions

1. Emphasis on _____ in the 1960s provided fertile soil for the growth of humanistic psychology.
   a. civil rights
   b. individuality
   c. communism
   d. laboratory rats

2. Which of the following is *not* a key element of humanistic psychology?
   a. personal responsibility
   b. identity crisis
   c. personal growth
   d. none of the above

3. Carl Rogers called individuals who are progressing toward an ultimate satisfying state of being
   a. fully functioning.
   b. self-actualized.
   c. self-centered.
   d. person-centered.

4. Which of the following is a characteristic of the fully functioning person?
   a. They are open to their experiences.
   b. They trust their own feelings.
   c. They pay attention to what is happening in the here and now.
   d. all of the above

5. When William approached the beautiful Carol and asked her out on a date, she laughed at him and then walked away. To handle this rejection, William convinced himself that Carol really didn't turn him down but rather she was laughing at something else. Which defense against anxiety does William's behavior illustrate?
   a. distortion
   b. denial
   c. displacement
   d. disorganization

6. When children adjust their behaviors in order to receive love and approval from their parents instead of disapproval, then children are experiencing
    a. conditional positive regard.
    b. unconditional positive regard.
    c. self-instructional training.
    d. a need for achievement.

7. If you were shipwrecked and landed on a tropical island, you most likely _____ first.
    a. look for inhabitants
    b. build a safe shelter
    c. establish a form of self-government
    d. look for food and fresh water

8. Among the common misconceptions of Maslow's need hierarchy is the assumption that
    a. all needs are included at some level in the need hierarchy.
    b. how well our lower needs are satisfied determines how much those needs influence our behavior.
    c. our lower needs must be completely satisfied before we can turn to higher needs.
    d. all cultures have the same basic need hierarchy.

9. Self-actualized people tend to
    a. accept other people for who they are.
    b. ignore their own weaknesses and focus on their personal strengths.
    c. be more spontaneous.
    d. be more greatly inhibited in their social interactions.

10. People lose their anxieties and experience a unity of self with the universe during
    a. moments of self-actualizing creativity.
    b. peak experiences.
    c. moments of emotional growth.
    d. optimal experiences.

11. When Csikszentmihalyi asked people to identify a moment when they felt most alive, participants in his study said that
    a. the task they were engaged in was challenging.
    b. the experience involved a task that demanded the person's full concentration.
    c. each step in the experience seemed to flow automatically to the next.
    d. all of the above

12. According to Rogers, the proper therapeutic relationship between therapist and client includes which of the following?
    a. unconditional positive regard
    b. unconscious impulses being revealed
    c. transference
    d. a peak experience during therapy

13. During person-centered therapy the therapist offers _____ of what the client seems to be saying.
    a. an analysis
    b. an interpretation
    c. a restatement
    d. suggestions for better thinking

14. Rogers believed that research into how people change during psychotherapy would help therapists
    a. estimate the limitations of their approach.
    b. become more sensitive to the needs of patients.
    c. uncover the parental influences on the personality.
    d. improve their ability to work with clients.

15. The use of the Q-Sort technique of personality assessment fits nicely with Rogers's theory of personality because
    a. clients must be told how to behave more appropriately by their therapist.
    b. therapists must help clients place the cards into the correct categories.
    c. clients discover the unrealistic ways in which they see themselves.
    d. clients know themselves best.

16. In a correlational analysis of Q-Sort responses, a zero correlation indicates that
    a. the client's real and ideal selves are identical.
    b. the client has no ideal self.
    c. the client's real and ideal selves are completely unrelated.
    d. none of the above

17. To some, humanistic psychology's reliance on the concept of free will to explain human behavior renders it
    a. extreme successful for helping people overcome their problems.
    b. unfit for scientific study.
    c. a viable approach for the 21st century.
    d. applicable in many areas of human experience.

Answers to Multiple Choice Questions

1.	b, 317	10.	b, 334
2.	b, 319	11.	d, 335
3.	a, 321	12.	a, 339
4.	d, 323	13.	c, 340
5.	b, 324	14.	d, 343
6.	a, 326	15.	d, 344
7.	d, 329	16.	c, 345
8.	c, 332	17.	b, 348
9.	c, 333		

Integrative Questions

1. If the humanistic approach to personality is the "third force" in American psychology, what were the first and second forces? Carefully contrast these "forces" by emphasizing their similarities and differences in theory, application, and assessment.

2. Contrast Rogers' view of human beings with Freud's conception of the person. Give an example of conditional positive regard and an example of unconditional positive regard.

3. Give an example of each level of Maslow's hierarchy of needs. Define enculturalization and peak experiences.

4. What makes people happy according to Csikszentmihalyi? Discuss the characteristics of optimal experiences.

5. Describe a typical person-centered therapeutic session in which the client is given the Q-Sort assessment. What are the general steps involved in the technique? What will the therapist discover about the client by using this technique?

Evaluative Questions

1. Consider the basic assumptions of humanistic psychology. Discuss the importance of a person's uniqueness in this approach to personality. Given that most personality researchers attempt to discover the underlying structure and basic influences on the personalities of all people rather than their uniqueness, how can humanistic psychology be considered a useful approach to personality?

2. Identify a person you know who is self-actualized or typically behaves in a self-actualized manner. What specific characteristics of this person point to self-actualization? Must the person in the example you gave have all the lower needs completely satisfied?

3. Describe an flow experience that you have had. How did you feel at the moment? Identify which of the eight components of optimal experience that you experienced in your example. Describe a plan for making your work tasks a source of happiness.

4. Suppose you were a manager in a large manufacturing company. Given what you now know about Maslow's theory of personality and the hierarchy of needs, what could you do to help satisfy the needs of your employees? If a worker said that she liked the money but was otherwise unhappy with her job, what would you want to know about the worker?

5. Consider the several criticisms of the humanistic approach. Do you agree with each criticism or do you feel that there still is a place in psychology for the humanistic view? What aspects of human nature are addressed by humanistic psychology that are not dealt with by any other approach?

Chapter **12**

The Humanistic Approach: Relevant Research

Chapter Outline

Self-Disclosure
    The Transparent Self
    Disclosure Reciprocity
    Self-Disclosure Among Friends and Romantic Partners
    Disclosing Men and Disclosing Women
    Self-Disclosure and Personal Adjustment
    Disclosing Traumatic Experiences
Loneliness
    Defining and Measuring Loneliness
    The Causes of Loneliness
        Negative Assessments of Self and Others
        Loneliness and Social Skills
Self-Esteem
    Self-Esteem and Reaction to Failure
        Low Self-Esteem and Failure
        Explaining the Different Reactions
    Self-Enhancement and Self-Protection Motives
    Self-Esteem Stability
    Self-Esteem and Culture
Need for Privacy and Solitude
    Time Alone
    Individual Differences in Preference for Solitude

Learning Objectives

1. Summarize the reasons for the initial interest in humanistic psychology and explain why critics of the approach call it soft psychology. List four concepts from humanistic psychology that have been highly researched.

2. Discuss the concept of self-disclosure and the implications for humanistic psychology of the research on self-disclosure. Explain the role it plays in the development of intimacy.

3. Specify the role of self-disclosure in personal adjustment according to Carl Rogers and to Sydney Jourard. Define the transparent self.

4. State the rule of disclosure reciprocity. Discuss Jourard's explanation for why we reciprocate disclosure intimacy and specify the relationship between self-disclosure and feelings of attraction and trust.

5. Give the status of the disclosure reciprocity rule for interactions among friends. Discuss self-disclosure between romantic partners. Describe how patterns of self-disclosure can vary as a function of gender.

6. Discuss how much self-disclosure is optimal for good personal adjustment. State the implications of the disclosure of traumatic experiences and emotional secrets for good physical and psychological health.

7. State the explanations humanistic and existential psychologists give for why loneliness is such a widespread problem in America.

8. Define loneliness. Contrast loneliness with isolation and give an example of each. Discuss some of the causes of loneliness and the characteristics of lonely people. and contrast the relative amount of self-disclosure between lonely and nonlonely people.

9. Distinguish between self-esteem and self-concept. Discuss the importance of self-esteem for humanistic psychologists. Distinguish between global and domain-specific self-esteem.

10. Compare how high self-esteem people and low self-esteem react to failure. Give reasons why these two kinds of people react differently.

11. Discuss the motives that distinguish high and low self-esteem people. Include in your discussion the roles of self-enhancement and self-protection. Explain how low self-esteem people use the self-handicapping strategy and the goal of its use.

12. Define self-esteem stability. Give reasons why some people have feelings about themselves that fluctuate while others feelings are more stable.

13. State the reasons why we should rethink our notions of self-esteem when working with other cultures. Discuss implications of different conceptualizations of the self in different cultures.

14. Give the humanistic psychology explanation for some people's desire to be alone. Discuss the research findings from studies of solitude, including how much people spend time alone and how they react to it. Contrast the drawbacks and benefits of time by oneself.

15. Define preference for solitude. Describe people at either end of this individual difference dimension. Discuss the method and results of Burger's research on preference for solitude.

Important Concepts

self-disclosure (p. 355)
dyadic effect (p. 357)
loneliness (p. 367)
feelings of self-worth (p. 373)
global self-esteem (p. 373)
self-enhancement (p. 377)
self-esteem stability (p. 379)
preference for solitude (p. 385)

disclosure reciprocity (p. 357)
disclosure flexibility (p. 361)
self-esteem (p. 373)
self-concept (p. 373)
domain-specific self-esteem (p. 373)
self-protection (p. 378)
self-handicapping (p. 378)

Programmed Review

In the early years humanistic psychologists argued that people cannot be reduced to a set of _____ .

numbers   p. 353

People engage in self-disclosure when they reveal _____ information about themselves to another person.

intimate   p. 355

Occasionally parents teach us the rules of social interaction directly, but often we are not aware of the _____ that teach us what is appropriate when interacting with others.

modeling/conditioning   p. 357

Self-disclosure may help people come to understand _____ better.

understand   p. 366

Loneliness occurs when a person's network of social relationships is _____ than the person desires.

smaller/less satisfying   p. 368

Given the opportunity to be in a conversation, lonely people tend to take on a _____ role.

passive interpersonal   p. 372

In contrast to low self-esteem people, when faced with failure people with high self-esteem typically work _____ as they do after successes.

just as hard   p. 374

Some researchers have proposed that people high in self-esteem are motivated by a concern for _____ .

self-enhancement   p. 377

In addition to individual differences in level of self esteem, people may differ in _____ .

self-esteem stability   p. 379

In Western societies the concept of high self-esteem is related to what one does to _____ oneself.

distinguish   p. 380

According to Maslow, people with a high need for privacy are not necessarily trying to _____ from relationships.

escape   p. 383

Multiple Choice Questions

1. Advocates of the _____ approach probably have generated less empirical research than psychologists from other approaches.
   a. biological
   b. behavioral/social learning
   c. humanistic
   d. trait

2. Making oneself "transparent" is the ultimate means of becoming
   a. more anxious.
   b. fully functioning.
   c. aware of the evaluations of others.
   d. all of the above

3. In a study of self-disclosure in which students took turns volunteering information about themselves, the students
   a. selected increasingly intimate topics.
   b. began with a discussion on trivial topics.
   c. tended to match their partners' level of intimacy.
   d. all of the above

4. Which of the following is true about conversations among good friends?
   a. There is little difference between the amount of self-disclosure with friends and with strangers.
   b. Familiar terms are not used very often.
   c. There are noticeable signs of intimacy that are lacking in conversations with strangers.
   d. There is more confusion over when to speak than in conversations with strangers.

5. In a study in which participants read about someone who was either highly disclosing or not very disclosing, the results showed that
   a. more participants thought the high discloser was a man.
   b. those who thought they were reading about a woman rated the person as better adjusted when she was disclosing.
   c. those who thought they were reading about a woman rated the person as better adjusted when she was not very disclosing.
   d. those who thought they were reading about a man rated the person as better adjusted when he was disclosing.

6. The ability to know when to talk about oneself and when to adapt one's level of disclosure is called
   a. traumatic disclosure.
   b. disclosure flexibility.
   c. disclosure adaptation.
   d. disclosure sensitivity.

7. Your best friend has been in an automobile accident in which others received serious injuries. According to research on disclosure of traumatic experiences, you suggest that your friend
   a. avoid talking about the accident until it seems right to do so.
   b. attempt to shut out any thoughts and feelings associated with the accident.
   c. talk about his or her feelings with friends or a trained therapist.
   d. write down any dreams he or she has for a month.

8. Loneliness has _____ on college campuses.
   a. become epidemic
   b. declined in the last decade
   c. increased slightly in recent years
   d. been estimated at 20% for freshmen

9. According to existential psychologists, loneliness is caused by
   a. guilt.
   b. questions of alienation and the meaning of life.
   c. conditions of isolation.
   d. poor social interaction and communication skills.

10. According to humanistic psychologists, one reason some people are chronically lonely is that they
    a. have a low need for Affiliation.
    b. avoid social contact.
    c. fear a loss of control.
    d. have negative assessments of themselves and of others.

11. Research tells us that one way each of us can help people who are lonely is to
    a. force them to interact in social settings.
    b. listen to them self-disclose.
    c. give them unconditional positive regard.
    d. teach them social skills.

12. A measure of domain-specific self-esteem is the
    a. Thematic Apperception Test.
    b. Tennessee Self Concept Scale.
    c. Q-Sort.
    d. Minnesota Self-Esteem Scale.

13. People low in self-esteem typically react to failure by
    a. losing their motivation.
    b. looking for excuses to which they can attribute their failure.
    c. making negative assessments of others.
    d. seeking psychotherapy.

14. When high self-esteem people are confronted with a negative evaluation, they
    a. easily blame others for the results.
    b. distort the outcome or deny the evaluation.
    c. begin to self-disclose at higher rates.
    d. tell themselves how well they do in other areas.

15. Lenny is anxious about his statistics assignment and so he waits until a high demand day in the computer lab to work on his assignment. He uses the lack of availability of computers as an excuse for not completing the assignment. Lenny's behavior illustrates the self-protection motive called
    a. passive-aggressive.
    b. symbolic behaviors.
    c. self-abasement.
    d. self-handicapping.

16. In order to measure self-esteem stability researchers have
    a. asked people to self-disclose.
    b. looked at how people respond to positive and negative feedback.
    c. asked people to regularly report their feelings of self-worth.
    d. all of the above

17. Results of research on time spent alone confirms the hypothesis that
    a. monks and other people who live in seclusion are more likely to be introverts.
    b. solitude becomes a less common experience with age.
    c. Americans spend a significant amount of time in solitude.
    d. Americans tend to be more socially anxious than members of other cultures.

Answers to Multiple Choice Questions

1. c, 353
2. b, 355
3. d, 357
4. c, 359
5. b, 360
6. b, 361
7. c, 366
8. a, 366
9. b, 367
10. d, 370
11. d, 372
12. b, 373
13. a, 374
14. d, 376
15. d, 378
16. c, 379
17. c, 383

Integrative Questions

1. Specify the several benefits to clients of psychotherapy from self-disclosing interactions. Give an example of disclosure reciprocity and discuss the circumstances and rules under which people self-disclose.

2. List the gender differences found in research on self-disclosure. Give one possible reason for each difference on your list.

3. State four reasons psychologists have shown a concern with loneliness. What other psychologists outside the humanistic approach have been concerned with loneliness?

4. Discuss the research findings on self-esteem. Specifically focus on the differences between people who are low and people who are high in self-esteem. How do these different personalities react to failures? Give a reason for this reaction.

5. How do people react to time alone? What factors determine whether an individual prefers solitude? Are there any benefits to spending time alone? If so, what are they?

Evaluative Questions

1. Choose two of the important questions for psychology given in the second paragraph on p. 355 of the Burger text. From your understanding of self-disclosure, answer these questions in your own words.

2. Why do we reciprocate disclosure of intimacy, according to Jourard? Are there other reasons for this behavior? Critically evaluate these reasons and give your own analysis of disclosure reciprocity.

3. Consider someone you know who seems lonely. What characteristics of lonely people are displayed in the person you are thinking about? State two ways in which you can help the person overcome feelings of loneliness.

4. Evaluate the differences in self-esteem for different cultures. What makes them different in this respect? For what purpose do we take questions and concepts of personality, like self-esteem, to other cultures for study?

5. Given that research indicates that interpersonal relationships are among the most important sources of happiness, why should some people desire their privacy? Give an answer to this question from the biological, trait, psychoanalytic, and humanistic approaches to personality. With which do you agree most? Support your answer.

Chapter **13**

The Behavioral/Social Learning Approach: Theory, Application, and Assessment

Chapter Outline

Behaviorism
Skinner's Radical Behaviorism
Basic Principles of Conditioning
    Classical Conditioning
    Operant Conditioning
        Shaping
        Generalization and Discrimination
Social Learning Theory
    Julian Rotter's Social Learning Theory
        Behavior Potential
        Expectancy
        Reinforcement Value
    Albert Bandura's Social-Cognitive Theory
        Reciprocal Determinism
        Cognitive Influences on Behavior
        Observational Learning
Application: Behavior Modification and Self-Efficacy Therapy
    Explaining Psychological Disorders
    Behavior Modification
        Classical Conditioning Applications
        Operant Conditioning Applications
    Self-Efficacy
Assessment: Behavior Observation Methods
    Direct Observation
    Self-Monitoring
    Observation by Others
    Self-Report Measures
Strengths and Criticisms of the Behavioral/Social Learning Approach

Learning Objectives

1. Define behaviorism. Describe John B. Watson's reasons for advocating that the subject matter of psychology should be overt behavior.

2. State Watson's definition of personality in your own words. Give the names and research findings of two scientists who influenced Watson.

3. Contrast the radical behaviorism of Skinner with the behaviorism of Watson. Explain what Skinner has said about personal freedom and dignity.

4. Describe the process of classical conditioning with your own example. Include the key components UCS, UCR, CS, and CR in your example. Use your example to illustrate second order conditioning and the limitations of classical conditioning.

5. State the law of effect and describe the nature of the observations made by Thorndike to formulate the law.

6. Define operant conditioning. Contrast operant conditioning and classical conditioning. Illustrate with your own examples two reinforcement strategies used in operant conditioning to increase desired behaviors.

7. Define extinction and punishment as two methods that can be used to decrease unwanted behaviors. Discuss the several limitations of each of these methods.

8. Give your own example of shaping. State the circumstances under which shaping is particularly useful. Define generalization and discrimination and give examples of two personality characteristics that could be explained by these processes.

9. Discuss the origins of social learning theory and explain how it expands upon the behavioral approach to personality. List the basic tenets of Rotter's theory, and discuss the relationships among behavior potential, expectancy, and reinforcement value.

10. Define reinforcement value. Recognize how different personality characteristics can be explained by differences in locus of control and reinforcement value.

11. Name the basic tenets of Bandura's social-cognitive theory and compare the theory with the strict behaviorist approach. Describe the reciprocal determinism model and discuss how the three parts of the model interact with examples of your own.

12. Define self-regulation and give examples of behavior that can be explained in the absence of external reinforcements and punishments.

13. Define observational learning and distinguish between learning and performance. Explain where our expectations come from for behaviors we have never performed before. Describe Bandura's experiment with nursery school children that investigated television and aggression.

14. Discuss how classical or operant conditioning could explain psychological disorders such as paranoia, aggression, and phobias. Describe how Watson used classical conditioning to create fear in a baby and how one might use classical conditioning to reduce such fear.

15. Define behavior modification. State the basic operant conditioning procedures typically used to change problem behaviors in individuals and groups.

16. Define self-efficacy and distinguish between outcome expectations and efficacy expectations. State why self-efficacy falls within the domain of social learning theory and list the four sources of efficacy expectations.

17. State three purposes of objective behavioral assessment. Summarize the principles of direct observation procedures. Define self-monitoring and state why it may be used as an alternative to direct observation. Describe the typical procedures used in self-monitoring and the disadvantages associated with its use.

18. Give reasons for the use of observation by others as a method of behavior assessment. State the nature of self-report measures of behavior. Evaluate which of the four basic methods of assessment can be used to monitor the progress of treatment.

19. Give the strengths of the behavioral/social learning approach to personality that has made it withstand the test of time. Discuss the advantages behavior modification procedures have over other therapy approaches.

20. State three limitations of the behavioral/social learning approach to personality. Distinguish among the criticisms given by humanistically and biologically oriented psychologists.

Important Concepts

behaviorism (p. 390)
radical behaviorism (p. 392)
classical conditioning (p. 394)
stimulus-response association (p. 394)
unconditioned stimulus (p. 395)
unconditioned response (p. 395)
conditioned stimulus (p. 395)
conditioned response (p. 395)
second-order conditioning (p. 395)
extinction (p. 396)
law of effect (p. 397)
operant conditioning (p. 397)
reinforcement (p. 397)
punishment (p. 397)
positive reinforcement (p. 397)
negative reinforcement (p. 397)
shaping (p. 399)

reinforcement value (p. 405)
social-cognitive theory (p. 406)
reciprocal determinism (p. 406)
potential environment (p. 407)
actual environment (p. 407)
self-regulation (p. 409)
observational learning (p. 409)
learning vs. performance (p. 409)
behavior modification (p. 413)
systematic desensitization (p. 414)
aversion therapy (p. 414)
token economy (p. 415)
biofeedback (p. 415)
self-efficacy (p. 416)
outcome expectation (p. 416)
efficacy expectation (p. 416)
performance accomplishments (p. 416)

generalization (p. 399)
discrimination (p. 400)
social learning theory (p. 401)
social behaviorism (p. 401)
behavior potential (p. 402)
expectancy (p. 402)
generalized expectancies (p. 404)
locus of control (p. 404)

vicarious experiences (p. 416)
verbal persuasion (p. 417)
emotional arousal (p. 417)
direct observation (p. 418)
self-monitoring (p. 420)
observation by others (p. 421)
self-report measures (p. 421)

Programmed Review

Watson argued that if psychology were to be a science, then psychologists must discontinue examining _____ .

mental states   p. 390

According to Watson, thinking was simply behavior he called "subvocal speech," evidenced by the movements of the _____ .

vocal cords   p. 390

Behaviorists believe that _____ can be examined to understand the processes that shape our personalities.

conditioning principles   p. 394

When an S-R association exists without conditioning, then the response in the association is called _____ .

an unconditioned response   p. 395

The process of using one conditioned S-R association to condition another S-R association is called _____ .

second-order conditioning   p. 395

When the consequence of a behavior increases the behavior's frequency, the consequence is _____ .

a reinforcement   p. 397

Although it is the most efficient method of decreasing undesired behavior, _____ is often a problem because people reinforce the undesired behavior without knowing it.

extinction   p. 398

Responding differently to rewarded and unrewarded stimuli is called _____ .

discrimination   p. 400

Arthur Staats introduced the notion of "behavior environment-behavior interactions" in his _____ theory.

social behaviorism   p. 401

A basic tenet of Rotter's social learning theory is that the strength of _____ is determined by the expectancy and value we place on reinforcement.

behavior potential   p. 402

Beliefs about whether or not our actions are likely to be reinforced or punished are called _____ .

generalized expectancies   p. 404

Bandura said that some of the most important causes of behavior, like thinking and symbolic processing, are capacities that are _____ .

distinctly human   p. 406

When there are no immediate reinforcements or punishments in the environment, Bandura argues that our actions are controlled by _____ .

self-regulation   p. 409

Many complex human behaviors cannot be learned through classical or operant conditioning but are acquired through _____ .

observational learning   p. 409

Using the principles of behaviorism to change problem behaviors is generally referred to as _____ .

behavior modification   p. 413

_____ is a treatment for problem behavior that uses classical conditioning to associate undesired responses with aversive images.

aversion therapy   p. 414

The behavior therapy called _____ requires special equipment that provides information about somatic processes such as muscle tension and heart rate.

biofeedback   p. 415

According to self-efficacy theory, how long people persist in their efforts to change their behavior is determined by _____ .

efficacy expectations   p. 416

In the method of behavioral assessment known as _____ sometimes therapists ask clients to role-play.

direct observation   p. 418

A benefit of the _____ method of behavior assessment is that clients are forced to pay attention to their problem behavior.

self-monitoring   p. 420

One advantage of behavior modification as an approach to therapy is the use of _____ and objective criteria for determining success or failure.

baseline data   p. 424

Multiple Choice Questions

1. According to the behavioral approach, personality is
    a. the result of inherited predispositions to behave in certain ways.
    b. a function of how we feel about conditions in the environment.
    c. the combination of environmental circumstances and unconscious impulses.
    d. the patterns of behavior we consistently engage in.

2. Social learning theory expands on behavioral accounts of personality to include
    a. nonobservable concepts like thought and perception.
    b. learning through observing other's behavior.
    c. learning by hearing about other's behavior.
    d. all of the above

3. The process used in Pavlov's famous demonstrations of learning became known to the scientific community as
    a. classical conditioning.
    b. operant conditioning.
    c. instrumental conditioning.
    d. behaviorism.

4. According to Skinner, when a person says they are talkative because they are happy, then
    a. happiness is the cause of the person's talkativeness.
    b. the person has only put a label on their talkativeness.
    c. the person has given an explanation of their talkativeness.
    d. talkativeness is the real cause of the person's happiness.

5. Laura is allergic to flowers and when she comes near a flower she starts to sneeze. She even sneezes when she is near artificial flowers. In terms of classical conditioning, artificial flowers are
    a. an unconditioned response to her allergy.
    b. an unconditioned stimulus for sneezing.
    c. a conditioned stimulus for sneezing.
    d. an unconditioned stimulus for her allergy.

6. From his observations of cats escaping from a "puzzle box" to obtain a piece of fish, Thorndike developed a theory that known as
    a. the law of operant conditioning.
    b. the law of effect.
    c. the law of consequences.
    d. the law of association.

7. George is stopped by a police officer after running a red light. After checking on George's driving record, the officer suspends his driving privileges. The officer is using _____ to modify George's behavior.
    a. positive reinforcement
    b. negative reinforcement
    c. punishment
    d. extinction

8. A baseball trainer works with a player to gradually improve his hitting with successive attempts to produce more hits each week of the season. The trainer is using
    a. stimulus generalization.
    b. discrimination.
    c. punishment.
    d. shaping.

9. Social learning theory developed out of behaviorism when many psychologists began to question
    a. whether the scope of behaviorism's subject matter was too limited.
    b. the usefulness of classical conditioning.
    c. the study of mental concepts.
    d. the assertion that operant conditioning is based on consequences.

10. According to Rotter, which of the following are psychological variables that must be considered to account for behavior?
    a. values
    b. expectancies
    c. perceptions
    d. all of the above

11. With respect to the locus of control continuum, Sally has an external orientation. Which of the following statements would she *least* likely make?
    a. "Hard work and perseverance pays off."
    b. "If my luck doesn't change, then I'll never get married."
    c. "I failed my psychology final because the professor doesn't like me."
    d. "If I die in a car crash, then it was my time."

12. In addition to external causes of behavior, Bandura argued that there are internal determinants as well. Which of the following is *not* an internal influence?
    a. experiences
    b. beliefs
    c. thoughts
    d. expectancies

13. From Bandura's research on observational learning in children we can conclude that whether a child performs an aggressive act depends on
    a. the amount of social encouragement the child has received to be aggressive.
    b. how extremely aggressive the behavior is.
    c. whether the model's behavior is reinforced or punished.
    d. whether the model is the child's parent.

14. The conditioned stimulus (CS) and unconditioned stimulus (UCS) in Watson and Rayner's experiment with a baby known as Little Albert were
    a. a white rat and a slap on the wrist.
    b. a loud noise and crying.
    c. fear responses and a loud noise.
    d. a white rat and a loud noise.

15. A treatment technique used to cure phobias by pairing images of the feared object with a relaxation response is called
    a. aversion therapy.
    b. aggression therapy.
    c. biofeedback.
    d. systematic desensitization.

16. According to the textbook, which of the following treatments for problem behaviors is an application of operant conditioning?
    a. aversion therapy.
    b. biofeedback.
    c. systematic desensitization.
    d. all of the above

17. One of the assumptions of self-efficacy theory is that there is a difference between believing that something can happen and believing that you can make it happen. The extent of people's beliefs that they can bring about outcomes is referred to as
    a. reinforcement value.
    b. efficacy expectation.
    c. outcome expectation.
    d. performance accomplishments.

18. Jill watches her roommate Melissa study every evening for two hours before watching television. She is aware that Melissa really doesn't mind studying once she has started and even seems to enjoy it. Jill forms an efficacy expectation that she also can study each night for a period of time based on
    a. vicarious experience.
    b. verbal persuasion.
    c. emotional arousal.
    d. none of the above

19. In their practice of psychotherapy, behavior therapists
    a. spend a great deal of effort uncovering the true cause of the client's problem.
    b. see overt behaviors as a sign of an underlying psychological problem.
    c. focus on observable behaviors without much reference to the underlying cause of the problem.
    d. attempt to determine the biological basis of some behaviors.

20. One problem with the self-monitoring method is that
    a. it cannot be used to assess the progress of treatment.
    b. the client may be dishonest about their behavior.
    c. the client is not a trained psychotherapist.
    d. it may be contaminated by self-report measures.

21. Which of the following is *not* a strength of the behavioral/social learning approach?
    a. The breadth of its description of human personality.
    b. Its solid foundation in empirical research.
    c. The usefulness of the therapeutic procedures based on it.
    d. The duration of behavior therapy compared to other approaches.

22. A criticism of the behavioral/social learning approach to personality is that
    a. behaviorists rejected free will as a determinant of behavior.
    b. the role of heredity is not given adequate attention.
    c. behavior therapists distort the real therapy issues in their narrow focus.
    d. all of the above

Answers to Multiple Choice Questions

1.	d, 390	11.	c, 404	21.	a, 424
2.	d, 390	12.	a, 406	22.	d, 425
3.	a, 392	13.	c, 411		
4.	b, 394	14.	d, 412		
5.	c, 395	15.	d, 414		
6.	b, 397	16.	b, 415		
7.	c, 397	17.	b, 416		
8.	d, 399	18.	a, 416		
9.	a, 401	19.	c, 418		
10.	d, 402	20.	b, 421		

Integrative Questions

1. In what specific ways does social learning theory provide a bridge between traditional behaviorism and more recent cognitive approaches to personality?

2. Why can it be said that Skinner's views of human behavior are like Freud's?

3. On what grounds can it be said that the behavioral/social learning theory approach to personality is similar to the trait approach? In what ways are these approaches distinct?

4. Contrast behavioral and social-cognitive explanations for why siblings growing up in the same home environment develop different personalities. How do these explanations differ from purely biological explanations of personality?

5. Bandura has said that behavior modification does not change people as much as it provides a method for people to change if they believe they can. Upon what assumptions is Bandura's idea based? Would a psychoanalyst or a humanist agree and why?

6. State the reasons for each of the procedures involved in direct behavior observation. How do these methods differ from assessment methods used in psychoanalysis?

7. What are the differences in the information of interest to psychoanalysts and behavior therapists when assessing problems?

8. How might a behavior therapist use direct observation and self-monitoring to determine an appropriate treatment for undesired behavior? Give your own example of a problem behavior and how to use these methods to achieve reliable assessments of the problem. What would take place in each method?

9. What were the basic empirical research findings of Watson, Skinner, Rotter, and Bandura? Give at least one unique contribution that each made to the behavioral/social learning approach to personality.

10. Contrast the following approaches to therapy in terms of the relative amount of time the treatment is expected to last: psychoanalytic, behavioral, and biological.

Evaluative Questions

1. What do you think of Watson's famous statement, "Give me a dozen healthy infants, well formed, and my own specified world to bring them up in, and I'll guarantee to take any one at random and train him to become any type of specialist I might select."? Give evidence from your understanding of personality to explain why you agree or disagree.

2. Most people understand that there is a connection between actions and consequences in shaping behavior. Since most people routinely rely on this understanding to shape other people's behavior, what is the justification of so much research on operant conditioning principles?

3. If you were a behavior therapist seeking to change the problem behaviors of a teenager, would you choose reinforcement or punishment? Why?

4. As you know there are a number of differences between radical behaviorism and social learning theory. Can social learning theory predict behavior better than the behavioral approach? If so, name several kinds of behaviors for which expectancy is a better predictor than experience.

5. State the usefulness of self-efficacy theory by discussing its advantages over behavior modification in explaining behavior problems. Speculate on the limitations of self-efficacy theory by giving an example of a behavior problem for which efficacy expectations have little impact.

6. Discuss the advantages and disadvantages of each of the four methods of behavior assessment in the behavioral/social learning approach. If you were a behavior therapist attempting to assess and treat a case of strong fear in a three-year-old child, which method of behavior assessment would you use and why?

7. Suppose you were a behavior therapist who adhered to social learning theory. A client is presented to you who suffers from symptoms of schizophrenia. Assuming there is a biological predisposition underlying the disorder, what are the relative advantages and disadvantages of using behavior modification procedures to help the person?

8. Give evidence from empirical research that illustrates a behavior for which the behavioral/social learning approach would have difficulty explaining. What charges have been leveled against behavior modification procedures with respect to their effects?

Chapter **14**

The Behavioral/Social Learning Approach: Relevant Research

Chapter Outline

Individual Differences in Gender-Role Behavior
    Masculinity-Femininity
    Androgyny
    Gender-Role Research
        Gender-Type and Psychological Adjustment
        Gender-Type and Interpersonal Relations
Observational Learning of Aggression
    Bandura's Four-Step Model
    Mass Media Aggression and Aggressive Behavior
Learned Helplessness
    Learning to Be Helpless
Learned Helplessness in Humans
    Some Applications of Learned Helplessness
        Learned Helplessness in the Elderly
        Learned Helplessness and Depression
Locus of Control
    Locus of Control and Personal Adjustment
        Psychological Disorders
        Achievement
        Psychotherapy
    Locus of Control and Health

Learning Objectives

1. State why traditional animal research in scientific psychology is not outside of the human condition.

2. Define gender roles. Describe the general processes by which different gender-role behaviors are acquired. Define the masculinity-femininity construct and state the two assumptions upon which this early scale was based.

3. Define androgyny. Explain how the androgyny concept challenged the assumptions of the masculinity-femininity approach and in what ways it increased our understanding of gender roles.

4. Name two widely used gender-role inventories. Distinguish among the sex-type categories into which researchers can place people based on these scales.

5. Describe three models that attempt to explain the relationship between gender-type and psychological adjustment. Summarize the research findings for each of these models. Give three general conclusions that can be drawn from research about the effects of gender-type on psychological health.

6. Give examples of research findings that support a relationship between gender-type and interpersonal relations. State the gender characteristics of the ideal marriage partner and three reasons suggested by research for why such characteristics are preferred.

7. Describe Bandura's Four-Step Model. Explain why each step is necessary for people to imitate aggressive behavior. Create a list of the circumstances under which people are more likely to imitate aggressive acts.

8. Discuss research findings on Mass Media Aggression that lead psychologists to believe that viewing aggression increases the likelihood of acting aggressively. State evidence for shortcomings in Bandura's Four-Step Model.

9. Define learned helplessness. Describe the classical conditioning research that led to the concept. State how dogs inappropriately generalized their learning.

10. Describe one research method used to test learned helplessness in humans. Specify the application of learned helplessness to two human problems and the solutions that research has suggested for each.

11. Define locus of control. Distinguish between internal and external locus of control. Name four behaviors that can be predicted fairly well from one's position along the locus of control dimension.

12. Interpret the research findings to determine whether it is psychologically better to have an internal or external locus of control orientation.

13. State the relationship between achievement and locus of control and give supporting research for the relationship.

14. Discuss what happens to a person's locus of control when undergoing therapy. State how the case of soldiers who experienced intense combat illustrated changes in locus of control.
15. Interpret the research findings to determine whether it is healthier to have an internal or external locus of control orientation. Discuss two differences in behavior that can account for individual differences in physical health.

Important Concepts

gender-role behavior (p. 430)
gender role socialization (p. 431)
masculinity-femininity (p. 433)
androgyny (p. 433)
undifferentiated (p. 434)
congruence model (p. 435)
androgyny model (p. 436)

masculinity model (p. 436)
observational learning (p. 440)
four-step model (p. 440)
learned helplessness (p. 448)
generalized expectancies (p. 454)
internal locus of control (p. 454)
external locus of control (p. 455)

Programmed Review

Behaviorists and social learning theorists maintain gender differences are the result of a lifelong process called _____ .

gender-role socialization   p. 431

Before the school years, children become aware of gender-role _____ mostly through their parents and peers.

expectations   p. 432

In addition to operant conditioning, it is clear that gender-role behaviors are acquired through _____ .

observational learning   p. 432

The fact that most people do not act is gender-appropriate ways illustrates that there are large _____ in the gender-role socialization of people.

individual differences   p. 432

125

The _____ model is the least supported explanation for how gender-type affects psychological adjustment.

congruence   p. 435

When people form first impressions of others, _____ is the gender-type liked by most people.

androgynous   p. 437

Many people view highly aggressive acts on a daily basis, but most do not rush out to find victims because people must _____ an aggressive act to be rewarded and not punishment.

expect   p. 440

The average 10-year-old in this country spends more hours watching television than in the _____ .

classroom   p. 443

In the first demonstrations of learned helplessness dogs were subjected to _____ with no escape.

electric shocks   p. 449

Learned helplessness in the elderly and in depressed persons often takes the form of a lack of _____ .

motivation   p. 452

Learned helplessness remains one of the leading models of _____ .

depression   p. 453

Research on locus of control was developed out of Rotter's concept of _____ .

generalized expectancies   p. 454

Young females suffering from eating disorders are likely to have an _____ locus of control orientation.

internal   p. 456

Behavior therapies that allow clients to administer their own rewards and punishments to stop smoking were more successful for people with an _____ orientation.

internal   p. 459

Multiple Choice Questions

1. With which of the following concepts is Rotter associated?
   a. learned helplessness
   b. observational learning of aggression
   c. classical conditioning
   d. locus of control

2. By which of the following processes does gender-role socialization take place?
   a. classical conditioning
   b. operant conditioning
   c. biological sex differentiation
   d. all of the above

3. Under which of the following categories would a person fall who scores low on both masculine and feminine scales of a gender-role inventory?
   a. androgynous
   b. masculine
   c. feminine
   d. undifferentiated

4. Sam and Sally are in a debate about gender roles. Sam says, "I think men should be masculine and women should be feminine." Sally disagrees and argues that the most well-adjusted people in society have the ability to respond with feminine or masculine behaviors depending on the situation. Sally agrees with which model?
   a. congruence model
   b. androgyny model
   c. masculinity model
   d. femininity model

5. All but which of the following is a reason why the most preferable partners in romantic relationships are feminine or androgynous people?
   a. their behavior emphasizes control and self-restraint
   b. they are better at expressing romantic feelings
   c. they are easy to talk to
   d. they have greater ability to resolve disputes

6. According to Bandura, if a person pays attention to a model's aggressive act and its consequences, and the person has the ability to enact what they have seen, then
    a. it is highly probable that the person will engage in the act.
    b. the person must also be able to remember the act to imitate it.
    c. outcome expectations matter little.
    d. performance has taken place but not learning.

7. Controlled laboratory research on observational learning of aggression requires participants to watch a violent or nonviolent program and then
    a. participants receive the opportunity to act aggressively.
    b. complete a questionnaire about their experience.
    c. engage in a group discussion of the program.
    d. take a test on their memory for details of the program.

8. Dogs exposed to an aversive stimulus from which they could not escape were found to
    a. learn through observation how to be helpless.
    b. avoid the stimulus on every trial.
    c. stop moving when placed in a shuttle-box situation.
    d. suffer from neurological damage.

9. Which of the following are ways in which humans can learn to be helpless?
    a. by being told they are helpless
    b. by observational learning
    c. by classical conditioning
    d. all of the above

10. Willy is a teenager who thinks that his swimming medals are the result of his effort. Mindy believes that her batting average in softball is the result of luck. Rotter would say that Willy has an _____ locus of control orientation and Mindy has a(n) _____ locus of control orientation.
    a. internal; external
    b. external; internal
    c. internal; generalized
    d. external; superstitious

11. In a study of suicidal patients, when asked to relive the events that took place before an attempted suicide the patients
    a. experienced terrifying flashbacks.
    b. described themselves in terms of an internal locus of control.
    c. described themselves in terms of an external locus of control.
    d. had no memory because the events had been repressed.

12. Studies of achievement have shown that external students
    a. perform better on academic tests than internals in elementary school.
    b. get better grades than internals in college.
    c. receive lower scores on achievement tests in high school.
    d. all of the above

13. Which of the following has been shown in research on assertiveness training?
    a. internal people showed little improvement
    b. external people showed significant improvement
    c. internal people felt their control over the training had been taken away
    d. all of the above

14. People with an internal locus of control may be more healthy than people with an external locus of control because
    a. internals do not concern themselves with the nature of illnesses.
    b. externals consume less healthy food and possess poor eating habits.
    c. internals tend to perform more preventative behaviors.
    d. externals cooperate with physicians more than internals.

Answers to Multiple Choice Questions

1. d, 430
2. b, 432
3. d, 434
4. b, 436
5. a, 438
6. b, 441
7. a, 445
8. c, 449
9. d, 451
10. a, 454
11. c, 458
12. c, 458
13. d, 459
14. c, 460

Integrative Questions

1. Now that you have studied the chapter, make a list of as many social problems or personal lifestyle issues that you can remember from the textbook. For each issue, what is the general research finding that can be applied toward its solution?

2. In what ways do stimulus generalization and discrimination contribute to the acquisition of gender-role behavior? Give an example of your own to illustrate your answer.

3. There are three explanations given in the textbook for how gender-type might affect psychological adjustment. What are these explanations and the research evidence supporting them? Are all three equally supported?

4. Describe the relationship between frustration and aggression in children. How does the behavioral/social learning explanation differ from that of Neo-Freudian theory (see Chapter 6)?

5. In what ways do outcome expectancy and efficacy expectancy play a role in Bandura's Four-Step Model? Give an example of an aggressive act that can be attended to, remembered, and enacted, but fails to have reinforcement value.

6. Contrast models of depression from the biological, humanistic, and social learning approaches. How might therapists with each of these orientations assess and treat people with depression?

7. Discuss the relationship between the constructs called learned helplessness and locus of control. Consider the research findings on elderly and depressed populations and state what aspects of these people's personality fit both constructs.

8. Humanistically-oriented therapists believe clients seeking help should be given complete control over the therapy. Based on the concept of locus of control, would a social learning theorist agree with this approach to treatment? Why or why not?

9. What role does Bandura's concept of efficacy expectations play in locus of control and physical health? Which group is more likely to have high efficacy expectations about their health, internals or externals? In contrast, how would a radical behaviorist explain the relationship between locus of control and health?

Evaluative Questions

1. Think of your many friends and acquaintances. Describe the behavior of two people you know, one male and one female, who seem to cross traditional gender roles. Include examples of their behavior that illustrate this reversal. Is it fair to say that in today's world with less gender restrictions there is little reason to conduct research on gender roles?

2. Some researchers believe that the characteristics underlying masculinity and femininity should be the focus of research rather than the traits masculinity and femininity. Do you agree? Why or why not? Given what you know about gender-role research, in what ways might such a change in focus contribute to our understanding of gender-role behavior?

3. Suppose a friend tells you that the happiest couples are those with one masculine member and one feminine member because these are complimentary traits. Based on the research evidence, would you agree? Is the belief held by your friend true for short-term relationships or long-term ones?

4. Now that you are familiar with the relevant research on observational learning of aggression, do you think it is likely that John Hinckley learned to try to assassinate President Reagan from repeatedly watching the movie *Taxi Driver*? Consider the likelihood of each step in the Four-Step Model and give research evidence to support your estimate.

5. Can it be said with some certainty that viewing aggression increases the likelihood of acting aggressively? For each research finding in support of this assertion state one alternative explanation for the evidence. Would you consider selling your television?

6. Learned helplessness has been explained by behaviorists that humans, like dogs, incorrectly generalize their helplessness to situations that they could control. How might this explanation for human learned helplessness differ from the perspective of a social learning theorist like Bandura? Why can it be said that it is often better to let the elderly take care of themselves?

7. How might an industrial psychologist apply the locus of control concept to increase productivity and job satisfaction? Give your own example.

8. If your mother told you that psychological disorders are caused by what people expect will happen to them, how might you respond? Could you say that problems in psychological adjustment are caused by external expectations?

Chapter **15**

The Cognitive Approach: Theory, Application, and Assessment

Chapter Outline

George Kelly's Personal Construct Theory
    Personal Construct Systems
    Psychological Problems
Cognitive Personality Variables
    Cognitive Structures
        Schemas
        Prototypes
    Cognitive Representations of the Self
        Self-Schemas
        Possible Selves
Application: Cognitive Psychotherapy
    Albert Ellis's Rational Emotive Therapy
    Self-Instructional Training
Assessment: The Rep Test
    Forms of the Rep Test
    Assumptions Underlying the Rep Test
    Clinical Analysis with the Rep Test
Strengths and Criticisms of the Cognitive Approach

Learning Objectives

1. Describe the emergence of the cognitive approach to personality and the early theorists within the approach.

2. Discuss the fundamental ideas underlying Kelly's personal construct theory. Explain the motivations behind behavior according to Kelly and define the concept of the personal construct and what is meant by range of convenience.

3. Give two reasons why one person's personality is different from another's according to Kelly's personal construct theory.

4. Discuss the application of personal construct theory to psychological problems such as anxiety. Give two reasons why our constructs sometimes fail us. State why construct systems may be incomplete.

5. Describe the development of research on cognitive personality variables. Define cognitive-affective units and discuss individual differences in terms of these units. Give three specific cognitive structures that are important in explaining personality.

6. Define schemas. Explain how these cognitive structures allow both stability and individual differences in personality.

7. Define prototypes. Describe the various functions of the prototype as a cognitive structure in personality.

8. Discuss the nature of the self-schema and how psychologists study hypothetical constructs like self-schemas. Discuss two functions of possible selves as cognitive structures.

9. Explain the importance of cognitive restructuring in cognitive approaches to psychotherapy. Discuss the therapist's role in this kind of therapy and contrast the approach with other kinds of therapy.

10. Describe the procedure called fixed-role therapy. Specify the elements of fixed-role therapy that make it a type of cognitive psychotherapy.

11. Discuss Albert Ellis's rational emotive therapy and highlight two goals of this cognitive approach to psychotherapy. Explain what is meant by the A-B-C process.

12. Describe the process of self-instructional training and identify its purpose.

13. Give the full name of the Rep test and explain its origin. Describe how the Rep test is used as a means of personality assessment and distinguish among various forms of it.

14. Give three strengths of the cognitive approach to personality. State how the cognitive approach improves on other approaches to personality.

15. State three criticisms or weaknesses that have been made of the cognitive approach to personality. Explain why some argue there is no need to introduce cognitive concepts in personality theory.

Important Concepts

man-as-scientist (p. 465)
personal constructs (p. 466)
superordinate personal constructs (p. 468)
subordinate personal constructs (p. 468)

template matching (p. 466)
range of convenience (p. 466)
anxiety (p. 470)
impermeable constructs (p. 470)

cognitive-affective units (p. 471)
schema (p. 473)
prototype (p. 474)
possible selves (p. 481)
fixed-role therapy (p. 483)
self-instructional training (p. 486)
Rep Test (p. 488)

cognitive structures (p. 473)
self-schema (p. 477)
particularistic self-schema (p. 478)
cognitive restructuring (p. 483)
rational emotive therapy (p. 484)
internal monologues (p. 487)
preemptive constructs (p. 490)

Programmed Review

The cognitive approach to personality explains differences in personality as differences in the way people _____ .

process information   p. 464

According to Kelly, people want to understand the world so that they can _____ what happens to them.

predict and control   p. 466

Kelly presented his theory of personality in a highly _____ manner.

organized and structured   p. 467

Those constructs that are more important than others in interpreting the world are called _____ personal constructs by Kelly.

superordinate   p. 468

Not only are there a limitless number of constructs we can use, the ways in which we can _____ these constructs are limitless as well.

organize   p. 469

Kelly suggested that the better we understand another person's _____ , the better we will get along.

construct system   p. 469

Kelly identified _____ as the "most common of all clinical commodities."

anxiety   p. 470

Mischel has argued that the events we encounter interact with a complex system of _____ .

cognitive-affective units   p. 471

_____ are hypothetical cognitive structures that help us perceive, organize, process, and utilize information.

Schemas   p. 473

We often use prototypes when judging whether a given object _____ in a cognitive category.

belongs   p. 474

When participants in a study of cognitive structures answered questions about themselves, they were more likely to _____ the information in the question.

remember   p. 479

_____ represent our dreams and aspirations as well as our fears and anxieties.

Possible selves   p. 482

Increased attention to cognitive structures has been paralleled by a growing interest in cognitive approaches to _____ .

psychotherapy   p. 483

According to Ellis, people have psychological problems because of faulty reasoning based on _____ .

irrational beliefs   p. 484

According to the cognitive approach to personality, one reason for recurrent problems is that some people typically engage in _____ thinking.

self-defeating   p. 487

In self-instructional training, therapists help clients prepare _____ for each step of the stressful experience.

internal monologues   p. 487

One assumption of the Rep test is that the constructs clients provide also apply to
_____ .

new people												p. 489

Cognitive personality theorists can be credited with taking the _____ approach one step further in explaining personality characteristics.

trait												p. 492

Multiple Choice Questions

1. One of the earliest psychologists to propose a cognitive model of personality was
    a. Carl Jung.
    b. Albert Bandura.
    c. Kurt Lewin.
    d. Walter Mischel.

2. To obtain a sense of predictability, Kelly suggests that we engage in
    a. template matching.
    b. scientific discovery.
    c. theory construction.
    d. hypothesis testing.

3. Which of the following is true about Kelly's fundamental postulate?
    a. He supported the psychoanalytic notion that past conflicts determine one's future actions.
    b. He believed that external stimuli are the basic influences on our behavior.
    c. He suggested that past experiences lead to constructs that help us anticipate events.
    d. all of the above

4. Which of the following corollaries suggests that a person decides for himself that alternative through which he anticipates the greater possibility for extension and definition of his system?
    a. construction corollary
    b. choice corollary
    c. organization corollary
    d. range corollary

5. According to Kelly, when constructs fail us as we try to predict events,
   a. old constructs are selected out of the system.
   b. failure to consider new information increases one's ability to make better predictions.
   c. new constructs are constantly generated to replace the old ones.
   d. we seldom accept it.

6. Within personal construct theory, anxiety occurs when
   a. one's construct system does not match the ideal system.
   b. one's constructs fail to become impermeable.
   c. we cannot predict future events.
   d. it becomes impossible to modify one's construct system.

7. Which of the following is true about the cognitive processes that produce behavior?
   a. Behaviorists argued that the situation is processed in the "black box."
   b. The processing that takes place between situation and response is of little importance.
   c. Cognitive-affective units are equally accessible from memory.
   d. Cognitive theorists acknowledge that the situation often initiates behavior.

8. It is clear that cognitive personality psychologists explain differences in personality in terms of
   a. differences in experience.
   b. differences in social settings.
   c. differences in mental representations.
   d. differences genetic makeup.

9. Which of the following is a function of prototypes?
   a. We use them to categorize objects.
   b. We use them to categorize people.
   c. they give us each a different way of perceiving the world.
   d. all of the above

10. Your self-schema consists of those aspects of your behavior that are
    a. unique to you and you alone.
    b. most important to you.
    c. similar to your parents and, by extension, your family.
    d. innate.

11. Many psychologists use methods such as _____ to study hypothetical constructs like the self-schema.
    a. timing mental processes
    b. self-report assessments
    c. dream analysis
    d. mental testing

12. In a study of processing information through the self-schema, participants were more likely to remember the information when
    a. words had the ability to generate emotions.
    b. the information was about participants themselves.
    c. a self-referent question was difficult to answer.
    d. participants had to generate a rhyme.

13. Results of research on the possible selves of juvenile delinquents indicates that
    a. only a few had developed a possible self of criminal.
    b. most had developed a possible self of rapist.
    c. many had developed possible selves for goals like having a job and doing well in school.
    d. more than one-third had developed a possible self of criminal.

14. Each kind of cognitive therapy identifies _____ as the cause of disorders.
    a. early childhood experiences
    b. a loss of the meaning of life and freedom
    c. inappropriate behaviors
    d. inappropriate thoughts

15. Which of the following is *not* among the methods used by Kelly in psychotherapy?
    a. asking people to clearly define their personal constructs
    b. asking people to describe their ideal self
    c. asking people to provide examples of their personal constructs
    d. forcing people to attend to their process of construing the world

16. Which of the following is an emotional Consequence?
    a. an invitation to go to the movies with a friend
    b. a feeling that a character in a movie could be real
    c. becoming frightened by a movie
    d. the thought that things that happen in movies happen to people

17. People can best prepare for and deal with potentially distressing situations through the cognitive therapy known as
    a. rational-emotive therapy.
    b. self-instructional training.
    c. fixed-role therapy.
    d. person-centered therapy.

18. Which of the following is true about self-instructional training?
    a. Its purpose is to replace self-defeating thoughts with more appropriate and positive ones.
    b. Through self-instructional training one modifies their own cognitive structures.
    c. It helps people overcome problems they are currently dealing with.
    d. both b and c

19. One of the goals of Kelly's Rep test is to better understand the client's
    a. reasons for feelings of anxiety or distress.
    b. unconscious impulses.
    c. interpretations of the world.
    d. self-schema.

20. In which of the following ways has the cognitive approach been criticized?
    a. Its has not been supported by enough research.
    b. It is not needed to explain individual differences in behavior.
    c. It has not added much to earlier approaches to personality.
    d. It does not fit well with current trends in psychology.

Answers to Multiple Choice Questions

1.	c, 464	11.	a, 479
2.	a, 466	12.	b, 480
3.	c, 467	13.	d, 482
4.	b, 467	14.	d, 483
5.	c, 469	15.	b, 483
6.	c, 470	16.	c, 484
7.	d, 471	17.	b, 486
8.	c, 473	18.	a, 487
9.	d, 474	19.	c, 489
10.	b, 477	20.	b, 493

Integrative Questions

1. Compare Kelly's conception of human personality with Freud's. Discuss the factors that influence personality and any similarities between the two conceptions. According to Kelly, how do we make predictions about the world?

2. How can personal constructs be used to explain personality differences? Make a list of the eleven corollaries proposed by Kelly and state what each means to you.

3. Discuss three personality phenomena that are explained by personal construct theory. Give an example of your own of an impermeable construct.

4. Discuss what is meant by the "black box." Contrast the cognitive approach to personality with the behavioral/social learning approach in terms of the black box. In what ways does cognitive theory improve on earlier explanations of situational influences on behavior?

5. Contrast cognitive psychotherapy with the approaches of Freud and Rogers. Use the methods of Kelly as an example of cognitive therapy in your discussion.

6. Contrast Kelly's approach to psychotherapy and Ellis's approach. What differences are in the goals of each approach? What assumptions are similar for each approach?

7. How do psychotherapists use the Rep test for clinical analysis? Define preemptive constructs and state what therapists should look for in the test.

Evaluative Questions

1. State in your own words Kelly's fundamental postulate. Critically evaluate the postulate based on your own experiences. In what ways were Kelly's ideas groundbreaking?

2. As suggested in the textbook, ask yourself what things you are interested in learning about people when you first meet them. Write down the first thoughts you have. Analyze your thoughts and interpret them as personal constructs. How do your constructs make your personality unique?

3. Give examples of cognitive structures that you have. Describe an example of a schema you have. State your prototypes for a friendly person, an athletic person, an intelligent person, and a nurturing person. Describe your own possible self.

4. If you could see your self-schema, what would it look like? Describe it in words or sketch it out like Figure 15.3 in the text. Give an example of a behavior that has become part of who you are. What concept in Allport's approach to personality is similar to the particularistic self-schema (see Chapter 7)?

5. Think of a strong emotional event that you have experienced recently. According to Ellis's approach to psychotherapy, identify the A, B, and C elements in your experience. Is your B element on the list in Table 15.3 of the text?

6. Why do some psychologists think of self-instructional training like an inoculation? Explain the goals of this type of therapy. State why psychologists believe this approach is promising.

Chapter **16**

The Cognitive Approach: Relevant Research

Chapter Outline

Androgyny Revisited: Gender Schema Theory
    Gender Schema Theory
        Evidence for Gender Schema Theory
    Continuing Issues
Cognitive Complexity
    Cognitive Complexity and Communication
    Cognitive Complexity and Coping with Stress
Depressive Schemas
    Cognitions and Depression
    Evidence for Depressive Schemas
Learned Helplessness Revisited: Attributional Model and Explanatory Style
    The Attributional Model of Learned Helplessness
    Explanatory Style
    Evidence for the Attributional Model

Learning Objectives

1. Define gender schema and describe gender schema theory. State who is sex-typed, the implications of being sex-typed or not, and how researchers go about studying differences in gender schemas.

2. Specify how sex-typed people process information along other dimensions than gender. Give evidence for gender schema theory.

3. Define cognitive complexity. Describe what psychologists have found about how cognitive complexity influences behavior and the cognitive complexity of children, therapists, and public figures.

4. Describe the relationship between cognitive complexity and communication skills. Describe the relative ability to cope with stress for people who have cognitive complexity. Discuss self-complexity and its relationship to coping behavior.
5. Explain how depressive thoughts are related to depressing feelings. Discuss the concept of a depressive schema and the research evidence supporting its existence.
6. Discuss the attributional model of learned helplessness. State why the animal model of learned helplessness was insufficient for understanding humans. Define hopelessness depression and contrast it with helplessness depression.
7. Define explanatory style. Discuss individual differences in explanatory style. Give examples of different attributions along the three dimensions.

Important Concepts

gender schema (p. 497)
cognitive complexity (p. 502)
hopelessness depression (p. 515)
attributional model of
    learned helplessness (p. 514)

self-complexity (p. 506)
depressive cognitive triad (p. 508)
depressive schema (p. 508)
explanatory style (p. 516)

Programmed Review

Putting a label on a style of behavior does not explain _____ the person acts the way they do.

why   p. 497

When a person organizes and stores information together in memory, psychologists expect to find this information to be _____ in recall.

clustered   p. 499

One way to demonstrate gender schema differences is to look at the _____ with which gender-related information is processed.

speed   p. 499

One difficulty facing gender schema researchers is that sex-typed people categorize information along dimensions besides _____ .

gender   p. 501

_____ refers to how elaborate or simple is a person's system of personal constructs.

Cognitive complexity   p. 502

Although some maintain that negative thoughts are a symptom of depression, the cognitive approach suggests that negative thoughts _____ depression.

cause   p. 508

Most people have an unrealistically _____ outlook on life.

positive   p. 509

Much of the evidence for depressive schemas comes from studies employing the _____ research techniques.

self-schema   p. 509

People processing information through a depressive schema have _____ to depressing memories.

greater access   p. 511

What we know about personality or any other area of psychology is the accumulated result of many _____ .

small discoveries   p. 513

According to the attributional model of learned helplessness, the explanations people give for their _____ determine whether learned helplessness develops.

lack of control   p. 514

Relatively stable patterns in the kinds of attributions people make are called one's _____ .

explanatory style   p. 516

Multiple Choice Questions

1. According to gender schema theory, a person is sex-typed if
   a. they are highly masculine.
   b. they are highly feminine.
   c. they are both highly masculine and highly feminine.
   d. either a or b

2. Because sex-typed and non-sex-typed people differ in the strength of their gender schemas, we should expect that
   a. sex-typed people describe behaviors as either masculine or feminine.
   b. non-sex-typed people recall gender-related information better.
   c. sex-typed people are less likely to notice inconsistencies in gender-related behavior.
   d. all of the above

3. In research on clustering and gender schemas, which of the following types of people were more likely to cluster words on a list according to gender?
   a. sex-typed
   b. cross-sex-typed
   c. androgynous
   d. undifferentiated

4. Which of the following is true if a person has cognitive complexity?
   a. As a child grows, the number of personal constructs remains relatively stable for each person.
   b. A psychotherapist is less likely to make biased diagnoses.
   c. These people are less likely to see the world in the same way others do.
   d. These people are less likely to be able to deal with ambiguity.

5. People high in cognitive complexity
   a. have more constructs with which to understand events.
   b. are less likely to become anxious when confronted with unexpected situations.
   c. are more sensitive to the perspective taken by another person.
   d. all of the above

6. One exception to the relationship between self-complexity and coping is that
   a. people who are low in complexity are more likely to become depressed, regardless of the their self-concept.
   b. high-complexity people are seldom able to cope with stress.
   c. low-complexity people have a more difficult time dealing with failure.
   d. a person whose high-complexity is made up of many undesirable facets is more prone to depression.

7. According to the cognitive approach to depression, processing information through the depressive schema
    a. causes people to become depressed.
    b. causes people to generate even more depressing thoughts.
    c. leads people to ignore positive information.
    d. all of the above

8. In research investigating the word recall of depressed people, which was *not* a group that recalled depression-related words better than normals?
    a. clinically depressed patients
    b. mildly depressed college students
    c. nondepressed patients
    d. students simple asked to think about some sad events

9. The simple model used to explain animal learned helplessness was inadequate for learned helplessness in humans because
    a. Humans always respond to uncontrollable situations with learned helplessness.
    b. Feelings of learned helplessness generalize to some tasks but not others.
    c. Conditioning often leads to learned helplessness in humans.
    d. Cognitive models of learned helplessness cannot be applied to animals.

10. Which of the following attributions tends to lead to learned helplessness?
    a. internal attributions
    b. unstable attributions
    c. specific attributions
    d. none of the above

11. Pessimists tend to have which explanatory style?
    a. external, stable, and specific
    b. external, stable, and global
    c. internal, stable, and global
    d. internal, unstable, and global

12. In a study of college students' reactions to their midterm grades, researchers found that
    a. only depressed students showed an increase in depressed mood immediately after getting negative feedback.
    b. nondepressed students with a specific explanatory style became depressed and remained so after two days.
    c. students in general showed an increase in depressed mood immediately after getting negative feedback.
    d. depressed students modified their explanatory style to be more specific.

Answers to Multiple Choice Questions

1. d, 497
2. a, 498
3. a, 499
4. b, 503
5. d, 506
6. d, 508
7. d, 509
8. c, 510
9. b, 513
10. a, 515
11. c, 516
12. c, 517

Integrative Questions

1. Discuss the basic ideas behind gender schema theory. What features of this theory make it clearly a cognitive theory? That is, how are cognitive personality theorists ideas incorporated into gender schema theory?

2. What are some of the continuing issues in the area of gender schema theory? Discuss the merits of some alternatives to the standard theory. What are the difficulties facing researchers in this area?

3. How does the depressive schema work? Contrast the outlook on life between most normal people and depressed individuals. Make a list of all the many predictions of depressive schema theory.

4. Contrast hopelessness depression with helplessness depression. How are they alike and what makes them different?

5. Why do internal-external attributions poorly predict depression? Give both a logical and a theoretical problem with the internal-external concept.

Evaluative Questions

1. Summarize and critically evaluate the several results of research on differences in gender schemas. List the various methods and consider alternative explanations for each result. Do you think you are sex-typed? Why or why not?

2. State whether depressed people process information through a specific depressive schema or simply through negative schemas in general. Give evidence from research to support your answer. What is the evidence from research on the accessibility of depressing memories?

3. Consider a situation in your recent past in which you failed to accomplish some task. From Table 16.1 on page 514 of the text, identify the kind of attribution you made about your failure. What implications does your attribution have in terms of your explanatory style?

Chapter **17**

Some Concluding Observations

Chapter Outline

Personality Theories as Tools
Personality Theory
    General Trends
        Signs of Growing Consensus
Personality Research
    Achievement
    Relationships
    Well-Being
    Health
Conclusion

Learning Objectives

1. Discuss the use of personality theory as an explanatory tool in everyday behavior. Explain why psychologists rarely find one agree-upon answer to questions of why people act the way they do.

2. Define what is meant by an "eclectic" approach in psychotherapy. State the reason many therapists identify themselves as eclectic.

3. Specify the general trends and current status of each of the major theoretical approaches to personality. State which continue in popularity and which are in decline.

4. Describe three signs of growing consensus among personality researchers.

5. Summarize the research and theory on achievement from various approaches to personality.
6. Summarize the research and theory on relationships and attraction from various approaches to personality.
7. Summarize the research and theory on the psychology of well-being from various approaches to personality.
8. Summarize the research and theory on behaviors related to one's physical health from various approaches to personality.

Important Concepts

eclectic (p. 522)
genetic influences (p. 524)

Programmed Review

Although each perspective on personality provides relevant information for describing human personality, no one perspective can give a _____ picture.

complete   p. 522

The number of traits identified by researchers and the test developed to measure these traits _____ .

continues to grow   p. 523

Today personality researchers have made a persuasive case that _____ cannot be easily ignored.

genetic influences   p. 524

Psychoanalytic, humanistic, and cognitive therapists generally work to help clients _____ their troubling thoughts.

bring to awareness   p. 525

Many researchers have examined _____ by looking at how people react to failure.

achievement behavior   p. 526

150

People who suffer from _____ want more social contact but often lack the skills necessary to establish satisfying relationships.

loneliness   p. 527

Multiple Choice Questions

1. The question for students of personality is not "Which theory is correct?" but rather
    a. "Which theory makes the most sense to me?"
    b. "How do the theories combine to give explain any given behavior?"
    c. "How can each approach to personality help me better understand behavior?"
    d. "Why do some perspectives fail to give the answers?"

2. One fact that points to the continued importance of the psychoanalytic approach is that
    a. neo-Freudian theories have not been able to replace it.
    b. the use of projective tests is still popular among therapists.
    c. the cognitive approach to personality has not achieved general acceptance.
    d. the only alternatives are the behavioral and humanistic approaches.

3. _____ has been in a steady state of transformation since it was established.
    a. The psychoanalytic approach
    b. Behaviorism
    c. Humanistic psychology
    d. Social learning theory

4. Today social learning theory is at times difficult to distinguish from
    a. humanistic psychology.
    b. the biological approach.
    c. the trait approach.
    d. the cognitive approach.

5. The current popularity of the _____ approach is a general trend that is reflected in courses in developmental psychology, social psychology, and abnormal psychology.
    a. cognitive
    b. biological
    c. social learning
    d. trait

6. One of the general ideas about the nature of human personality that is gaining acceptance among theorists from all perspectives is
   a. the importance of thoughts outside of awareness.
   b. the genetic influences on personality.
   c. the interaction between the person and the situation.
   d. all of the above

7. In Western cultures, how satisfied people are with their lives tends to be a function of
   a. childhood experiences.
   b. genetic influences.
   c. self-esteem.
   d. personal constructs.

8. Studies of _____ indicate that internals and externals typically have different ideas about their role in maintaining physical health.
   a. attributional style
   b. self-schemas
   c. extraversion
   d. locus of control

Answers to Multiple Choice Questions

1. c, 522
2. b, 522
3. b, 523
4. d, 523
5. a, 524
6. d, 525
7. c, 528
8. d, 529

Integrative Questions

1. Discuss three general ideas acknowledged by theorists from different perspectives that represent a growing consensus in personality research and theory.
2. Indicate how different approaches to personality integrate to give us a better understanding of behaviors related to achievement, relationships, well-being, and physical health.

Evaluative Questions

1. Think of an everyday question you have about people and their behavior (i.e., like the question in the text: Why do people keep pets?). Use personality theory as a tool to understand the answer to your question. List six theoretical perspectives and state what theorists within each approach would say about the behavior of people in your question.

2. Summarize the current status of each of the major theoretical approaches to personality. With which do you most agree? Support your answer.

3. Speculate about the future of personality research and theory. Given what you know about current trends in psychology and the rapid changes in our society, what do you think the future picture is like? Is it possible that some of the established perspectives will merge? If so, in what ways do you think they will come together?